LOVING CONFRONTATION

Beverly Caruso

BETHANY HOUSE PUBLISHERS

MINNEAPOLIS, MINNESOTA 55438

A Division of Bethany Fellowship, Inc.

Published by Bethany House Publishers
A Division of Bethany Fellowship, Inc.
6820 Auto Club Road, Minneapolis, Minnesota 55438

Printed in the United States of America

Library of Congress Cataloging-in-Publication Data

Caruso, Beverly.
    Loving confrontation.

    1. Christian life—Pentecostal authors. 2. Inter-personal rela-
tions—Religious aspects—Christianity.
I. Title.
BV4501.2.C3365   1988   248.4'8994   88–19453
ISBN 1-55661-020-3

LOVING
CONFRONTATION

ACKNOWLEDGMENTS

This book is for . . .
>   those Christians who long to apply God's Word to their relationships.

It is about . . .
>   real people, whom I know and love dearly, who accepted the challenge to share our lives together—God's way. For their sakes, I've changed the identities of some.

With special thanks . . .
>   to John and Tibby Sherrill who encouraged me to share these concepts,
>   to my friends Janet Benge, Libby Bordewich, Ken Marks and Janny Rogers who gave valued suggestions,
>   and to David Hazard who diligently polished my efforts.

With love . . .
>   to our children, Debbie, Mike and Dave, who never revealed their weariness of my preoccupation with this writing, but rather encouraged me, and covered for me . . . at the stove, with the vacuum and even washing windows,
>   and to our grandchildren, Daniel, Katie and Elizabeth who forfeited fun times with "Nonna."

With deep gratitude to . . .
>   my best friend—my husband Pete—who long ago saw potential in a timid young woman; he believed in me, loved me, praised me and encouraged me—until I believed in myself enough to see this writing to completion.

In memory of . . .
>   Raynor Nicholson who affirmed my first attempts at writing. He lived these principles among us. We miss him so!

BEVERLY CARUSO is the wife of Peter Caruso, an Assemblies of God minister. Together they pioneered and pastored the Olive Assembly of God in Orange, California (1961–1982), which trained and sent out 70 full-time Christian workers. Her international ministry has been both as a counselor and teacher/speaker—marriage enrichment seminars, retreats and conferences, as well as singles and pastors seminars. Their family includes three children as well as grandchildren, and they are currently establishing the New Life Community Church.

FOREWORD

I t has been nearly twenty years since I first met the Carusos. I have often stayed in their home, ministered in their church, and shared fellowship with them in conferences across this nation. Little did I imagine on our first meeting that Beverly would come into a ministry that would warrant writing about, but she certainly has, and what she shares can enable us to learn from her experience rather than having to go through such things for ourselves.

When the space shuttle *Challenger* exploded just seconds into its flight, NASA was forced back to basics. Perhaps the present-day church, which seems to have so many explosive failures in its programs and developments, needs to get back to basics, too. Maybe our enthusiasm to explore newer truths has caused us to become careless with the fundamentals that make the Christian life work. Potentially, we may have become so preoccupied with progress that we have ignored Bible principles.

Is it possible that a book written for an Eastern culture many hundreds of years ago could contain life principles that would work in our Western industrialized culture? Pete and Beverly Caruso thought so, and they taught those principles to the congregation they pastored. Initially these concepts seemed simplistic, but when the people began to act the principles out, they became revolutionary. Lives were changed, marriages were saved, relationships were strengthened, and unbelievers were attracted to Christ.

As case history after case history is unfolded in the book, the reader shifts from amazement that these principles work to wondering why we ever doubted that what Jesus taught was both practical and applicable to all generations. Love, forgiveness, confrontation, and submission are principles a Christian society dare not ignore, for they are foundational to relationships both with one another and with God.

The principles seem daring—dare we try them? Perhaps we need to remind ourselves, "If all else fails, read the instructions." This is an instruction book.

Judson Cornwall

CONTENTS

THE DELICATE LINE BETWEEN TRUTH AND LOVE....

T he relationships we form with Christian brothers and sisters often cause us to tread upon fine lines.

In some cases, the people we love "in the Lord" can seem closer to us than our own flesh-and-blood. We look to our circle of Christian friends for support, prayer, and closeness. We sometimes open ourselves to them, unburdening our souls. At the same time, we're not blind to human flaws. The same good people at the Bible study or in the next pew may knowingly or unknowingly let us down, wound, or betray us. Our dearest Christian friends can sometimes be the greatest source of irritation and gossip. Or we ourselves can become aware that a Christian friend is putting on a good appearance at church when his conduct at home or on the job is dreadful.

For Christians, close relationships present some touchy problems.

Some believe that we should always "speak the truth in love"—even if it's hurtful. People like this seem to thrive on confrontation. If the person being confronted is insulted or left in tears, they say, "I had to tell it like it is. I can't lie."

Others take the position that noticing the fault or sin of a brother in the Lord is "judging." These people say, "All I know is that Jesus Christ forgave my sins. 'Let him who is without sin cast the first stone.' " They say that Christians should always love, always overlook the sins of another and just forgive.

Most of us bounce back and forth over this delicate line between what we call "truth" and what we call "love," never sure which side we should be on in any given situation. I was one of those "bouncers." Because my husband, Pete, was a church pastor, that made me a pastor's wife— one of the worst positions to be in when you are the one hearing about the aches in every joint!

For years, I acted as a dumping ground for complaints, gossip, arguments. To be honest, I probably did some dumping of my own, too. The whole area of building right relationships was difficult to grasp. I knew what the Scriptures said— or so I thought—but the relationships I was in or knew about were more complicated than relationships in Jesus' day, weren't they? Relationship problems tended to slide.

It was a major turning point in the life of our church when we decided to risk believing that

Jesus' words are true. We dared to believe that Christian relationships can be built strong, that "fractures" can be healed, not merely covered up, that delicate situations and fragile people can be handled without destroying privacy and personal integrity.

I'll be honest right up front and say it wasn't easy, and we are still working at learning all that the Scriptures direct us to do in our relationships with others in the body of Christ. But we have seen the amazing impact on a whole congregation when we decided to become doers of Jesus' words and not hearers only.

The purpose of this book is to teach and encourage, not to tell the story of our church. But because my learning experiences with relationships are so intricately bound up with that particular congregation, that's where I feel I must start . . . beginning with the day I got plain fed up.

CHAPTER ONE

"THIS IS NO PICNIC"

I added cups and plates to the box of picnic supplies, then walked into the front room to look out the window. Outside, the usual southern California smog had been blown off by winds during the night. The sky was clear and sunny. It was a picturesque spring day, perfect for our church's first outing of the year.

Then why did I have a nagging uneasiness about this get-together?

Pete hadn't told me of any hardships or crises among our 150-member "flock," most of whom lived near us in our small, suburban community of Olive, part of the city of Orange. This was to be a relaxed day, full of fun. Our three children were already outside, with football, frisbee and skateboard in hand. After the picnic, there would be volleyball and other games. The only cloudiness about the day was the vague anxiety that skittered across my thoughts.

Pete strolled into the kitchen just then to carry the heavy box out to the car for me. "Are you all set, Hon?"

I smiled at him. I'm pretty much the level-headed sort. As a pastor's wife of more than ten years, I'd learned to "roll" with a lot of punches, and was not one to give in to fleeting mood-swings. "All set."

When we unloaded the car at our nearby park, I was distracted by the heady scent of orange blossoms carried across the lake on a breeze. Some of the "early birds" had picked a site on a shady knoll overlooking the open playground. Pete went off with some men from the church, the kids darted to the playground, and I was soon settled in a folding lawn chair beside two other women.

I'd come into the picture midstream in their conversation, which they resumed the moment our greetings were through.

"Like I said before," one of them picked up, "she never comes prepared to teach that Sunday school class."

"I don't think that's the problem," the other responded. "From what I hear, she talks down to the children. I think she just doesn't understand kids that age."

At some point, I felt pulled into the conversation. Part of me felt obliged to offer some kind of solution—after all, I was the pastor's wife. "Maybe we should get a new teacher for that age group," I offered weakly.

When the conversation moved on to other things, I felt relieved. By noon, when we crowded into line at the picnic tables for the potluck lunch, the Sunday school dilemma was forgotten. Happily, I chatted with others as we moved down the tables. I was starving. My paper plate held small samplings of hot chicken dishes, casseroles and salads.

Halfway through the line, a loud blast cut through our light banter.

Thirty feet away, Art, a man I had a hard time relating to, loomed over his small son, who looked up at him in wide-eyed terror. Art's red beard seemed to bristle as he bellowed again. "I told you not to get off that blanket!"

The little boy backed fearfully toward the blanket, where his sisters sat, wooden and expressionless as toy soldiers. Penny, Art's slender wife, moved silently to the blanket, avoiding our eyes. Her little ones huddled around her. It wasn't the first time we'd witnessed a public tirade like this.

She's sacrificing her personhood, the thought sizzled inside me, *in order to keep peace in that family.* I stopped myself from going further. It seemed lately that just the sight of Art brought a rush of thoughts that bordered on judgments about him—or had I already secretly crossed that border in my heart?

Having been told that my face is an open book, I furiously studied the over-full paper plate in my hands. Art's shouting had parted the peaceful atmosphere like a boulder dropped in a pond, and now the lunch-line conversation closed over the intrusion, swallowing his anger in polite pretense that we hadn't noticed.

When I found my way to the shady seat again, the chicken and salads looked unappetizing. My stomach was in knots.

Following lunch, while babies snoozed on blankets and the volleyball tournament was underway, I accompanied several women on a walk along park trails. We passed some swings where young mothers were rhythmically pushing their tots. One of my companions surprised me by asking, out of the blue, "How is a woman supposed to submit to her husband if he's a lousy husband?

"I mean," she hurried on, obviously aiming her questions at me, "he never helps discipline the kids. He expects me to balance the checkbook, yet he buys whatever he wants without a thought about our finances . . ."

She was on a roll now, giving us a long list of irritations and hurts. I sensed she'd been waiting for this moment, away from her husband, to unload. What else could I do but listen with a concerned expression and nod?

What else, indeed. When she was finished, she and the other women paced along silently beside me. I felt them waiting for my response. How I hated that feeling!

I cannot remember now what I told them— a few Scripture verses and probably some advice I'd heard from someone else. I only recall that it sounded thin and inadequate. And I was amazed that, after so many years as a Christian, I didn't have something more concrete and helpful to say.

She must have realized I had little to offer in

this matter. When we reached the point where the stream pours into the lake, she turned her attention to a group of children who were feeding dry bread to some ducks.

Late that afternoon, when the desserts were gone and the final round of volleyball was over, Pete drove us home. I leaned back in the seat, feeling exhausted. More than that. I wished I'd never have to go to another church picnic as long as I lived.

At home that evening, Pete asked. "What's on your mind, honey?"

He found out in a hurry. I reminded him of Art's angry outburst, filled him in on the complaints about the Sunday-school teacher and the woman who was disillusioned with her marriage. All afternoon, almost until we'd climbed into the car again, I'd heard about people's gripes and squabbles.

"I get so tired of it," I finished.

He shook his head. "It's your *job* to listen, Honey. If you don't listen to it, they'll only talk about it to someone else, and then it's gossip. You can't let it weigh you down. Just learn to let it go in one ear and out the other."

Pete's advice to me that day was not the sum total of our wisdom about handling relationship problems among Christians. We knew there were specific directives from Jesus, Paul, and the other New Testament writers. The truth is, we just didn't see in those days that building healthy relationships was a high priority for establishing and maintaining the health of a church. We had built our ministry on what Pete had learned in Bible college and, of course, we mimicked the example of churches we'd attended before launching the church in Olive. So we relied on the common methods of pastoral care—preaching, teaching and church programs—hoping those in our "flock" would get enough feeding on Sundays to keep them strong through the week.

But the serious relationship problems that surfaced the day of the picnic were not unusual. *No* church or personal relationship is going to be problem-free. The mistake we sometimes make as Christians is to imagine that we can live in this world without conflict. Then, the moment another Christian rubs us the wrong way, we're shocked, dismayed, offended.

Some people, unfortunately, escalate the problem to an unbelievable degree, developing a sort of "spiritual" chip on their shoulder. When you ask them about the offense, they say, "Well, I never expected *Christians* to act that way. I don't think I'll ever trust another Christian again." To me, this is a symptom of two things: first, the unrealistic expectation that others should never upset us and that we will never hurt others; second, a lack of understanding as to what the Scriptures say about handling conflict.

What is lacking for many of us is not conflict—heaven knows!—but Christian *maturity* that comes from an understanding of how to apply biblical principles to our relationships.

That was the thing that had troubled Pete

and me even before the church picnic. We just did not see the spiritual maturity in the members of our church—or in ourselves—that we longed for. In hindsight, we see now that we had mistaken *knowledge* of the Bible, which we weren't lacking, for *application* of biblical principles. So, like Christian folks everywhere I suppose, we all got along fine during the Sunday service, then ran into a lot of irritations with each other the rest of the week.

And *that,* I decided after Pete's "in-one-ear-and-out-the-other" advice, had to change.

All during the next week, Pete and I took a hard look at the real weakness of Christian relationships in our church. Pete, who is very much an action-oriented leader, decided to take some immediate steps to point out the need we all shared, which was the need for mature relationships built on scriptural principles.

The first principle Pete called our attention to, in a sermon the very next Sunday, was from Matthew 18. Here, Jesus says that if a brother sins against us, we must go to him first before we talk about the offense to all our other friends.

To be truthful, I sat fidgeting in the pew as he spoke. Before we see how to put the Matthew 18 passage to work, which we will in Chapter 2, I must focus on the real foundational principle for building fruitful Christian relationships.

As Pete preached, I thought, *This will never work. It's idealistic and impractical. All this is going to do is get people mad at each other. And then our counseling load will double!* In my head were scenes of the warfare I imagined as a result of putting this scripture into practice.

That's when I found myself face-to-face with the first wrong relationship that had to be dealt with—my own loose handling of Jesus' living word in the Scriptures. To put it bluntly, I was confronted with my own sin of unbelief. I saw it so clearly in my negative attitude and judging Jesus' words as too simplistic.

The first principle, then, in building fruitful Christian relationships is to take God at His word. You may shrug that off as too simple even to mention. But it's far easier said than done.

I could imagine, for example, having someone come to me to point out a blunder of mine. Though I don't enjoy being embarrassed or having to admit I was wrong, it would not be too difficult for me to ask their forgiveness.

But what if someone came to me with a complaint about a third party? Could I resist the temptation to get the "inside story"—which can be disguised as "counseling"? Did I dare to trust in Jesus' directive to send that person back to the offender? That morning sitting in the pew, I knew that I was usually weak and *not* bold enough.

There were many other questions we all faced in the days immediately following Pete's challenge. What are the biblical principles that should shape and direct our relationships? More challenging, how do we apply those principles in everyday life—in real situations involving real people?

These are just some of the relationship questions that we faced together as brothers and sisters as we began an experiment in Christian living. It was not without its risky moments. But it shook and renewed our leaders, our marriages and personal friendships.

What we discovered by taking God at His word transformed our relationships as a body of believers. We found new ways to break through barriers that we didn't even know existed between us as we sat side-by-side at Bible studies or in the pews or chatted over coffee. The result was a depth of commitment to bearing one another's burdens, sharing in the joys and hurts, building a community of believers that was to become an attractive light to searching people all around us. In other words, we moved many steps closer to the way Jesus promised we Christians could live with each other.

I don't want to imply for a minute that you should begin where we began or reach the same goals we did. My real intent is to teach and encourage, not to hold up our experience as a model. So if you are longing for deeper relationships, the kind that can withstand strains, the kind that can be relied on in tough times, I offer a challenge.

Start right now by making a commitment in prayer to take God at His word. As we examine the biblical principles put forth on these pages, apply them to your own relationships. Search the Scriptures for others that relate to your situation. Share your thoughts and convictions with your spouse, a Christian friend, your Bible study or prayer group.

I can assure you that you will see the fruit of the Spirit—love, joy, peace, patience, and all the rest—begin to reshape your life and the lives of those around you. Because, as someone has said, "You and God make a majority." Your commitment to living God's way can and will make a powerful impact on all those whose lives you touch.

CHAPTER TWO

"GO TO YOUR BROTHER . . ."

If your brother sins against you, go and show him his fault, just between the two of you. . . . If he refuses to listen, take one or two others along. . . . If he refuses to listen to them, tell it to the church. (Matt. 18:15–17, NIV)

As I mentioned in the first chapter, the hope of living in "bumpless," "bruiseless" relationships is unrealistic. To expect that our spouse, our children, our pastor, or Christian friends won't ever upset us is a false hope. Jesus never promised us perfectly smooth relationships, but to handle the bumps and bruises that inevitably come, He did give us this simple directive in Matthew 18.

At least upon first glance it seems simple. On the surface, we see that this scripture applies in two situations: when someone has offended you personally, and when someone comes to you to complain about a third party. In the first case, we are told to go to the offender ourselves. In the second case, we should send the complaining party to the offender.

If we're honest, though, most of us would probably admit that we have a great deal of trouble applying Jesus' clear command in either case. Why is that so?

Let's examine the first situation—in which you're the person who's been offended—by using an illustration.

Let's say that you have asked Bob, one of your closest friends, to pray about a very touchy family problem. The information was shared in private and you made it clear that it was purely confidential. Two days later, however, you bump into another acquaintance on the street, and he says, "I'm so sorry to hear about what's going on in your family. Is there anything I can do to help?"

Immediately, you're reacting inside, aren't you? You're positive the information could have come from only one source. You feel hurt, angry. I'm not saying that you're wrong to have these feelings. The Apostle Paul said, "Be angry, and sin not" (Eph. 4:26, KJV). Yes, even as Christians we can and will feel anger. It's the "sin not" part we need to be concerned about!

Hot on the heels of your inner angry reaction, you also have an outward reaction. You storm off to find the nearest phone and call Alice, another close friend. Without divulging details, you pour out your hurt to her. "Can you believe that Bob would betray me like that? All this time I thought he was a man of honor. I guess he isn't the kind of person you can trust!"

What complaining to Alice has accomplished is to enlist her on your side against Bob. What you were saying, without voicing it openly, was, "I'm mad and I don't trust him—and you shouldn't either!" The net effect is that you've judged Bob and even entered into character assassination.

It is so sad that we Christians so often enter into this kind of sin against our pastors, their wives, our own spouses, and other Christians. We may call it "sharing," "seeking counsel," or "asking for prayer." And in some cases we do need the advice and prayers of others. But not before we have done what Jesus asks us to do—go to our brother.

The secret to success in this kind of situation is to go to your brother or sister in a right spirit. How do we prepare our hearts for this?

The first, and probably the most important thing we are to do is to examine our own heart. In the Sermon on the Mount, Jesus told the people gathered to hear Him that they should take care of the "plank" in their own eye before trying to remove the "speck of sawdust" from their brother's eye. So, too, we need to ask God to show us if our vision has been blurred by the irritations that blow our way.

After our spirit has been cleansed, we can ask God to fill our hearts with the right attitude toward the one who offended us. We must guard against going with an aggressiveness that communicates: "I'm right, you're wrong, and I'm coming to set you straight!" Instead, we should communicate a heart attitude that says: "I'm eager to hear what you have to say."

Just before approaching a person with whom I need to discuss a hurt or disagreement, I make it a point to sit down and read 1 Corinthians 13, the "Love Chapter." In fact, I read it several times, with the face of my brother or sister in mind. The more I see them in the light of God's love, the more love seems to flow into my heart for them. Then I can go with an attitude that wants to affirm.

Now let me immediately explain what I mean by affirmation.

Some of us who don't like confrontation at all (and I fall into this category) have a tendency to try to smooth conflict over before we've gotten to the root of it. Affirmation doesn't mean starting off with a list of compliments. Maybe you've had a friend launch into a long catalog of your "good points," with the uncomfortable sense that you know what's coming. You're being fattened for the kill. This approach actually makes you feel wary and ready to defend yourself.

Rather, you should begin by underscoring these two things: your commitment to the individual and to the relationship; your eagerness to listen to their viewpoint. This will affirm your friend's value at a much deeper level than a listing of favors they've done or characteristics that you like about them.

Then, I simply go ahead and explain the way I view the circumstances about which I'm bothered. At this point, it's wise to *stick to the facts*, reconstructing the events and what was said as clearly as you can recall. Along with listing the outward circumstances, it's also fair to state how the circumstances made you feel. Never attack ("You did that just to hurt me"). Never judge and label ("You're the biggest gossip I know"). Simply state your inner response ("It hurt me. In fact, I got angry").

Your conversation should have two aims. First, to get at the truth. As 1 Cor. 13:6 says, "Love does not delight in evil, but rejoices with the truth" (NIV). And the reason for getting at the truth is not to assign blame, which is our human tendency, but to make way for the second aim—reconciliation. That, Paul tells us in 2 Cor. 5:18, is a calling all Christians share in.

Now let's reverse the situation we looked at earlier. Let's say that a friend comes to you to complain about Bob's offense.

You might listen to the complainer to be polite or because you are sympathetic. Or you might argue on Bob's behalf. Or you might offer counsel and prayer for your wounded friend. Some people— too many of us, I suspect—listen to complaints about Christian friends all the time, but for wrong reasons. Most of us have learned that knowledge is power, and it gives us a feeling of importance to have "inside" information. Others feel that it would be insensitive to turn away someone who is hurt and upset.

What is our response to be? Far from turning a cold shoulder to a friend or washing our hands of the problem, we are to play a vital part in healing wounds in the body of Christ. This is what we began to find in the weeks following Pete's first challenge from the pulpit. After my own first-step decision to start taking God at His word, it wasn't long before that resolve was tested.

I'd just finished teaching a women's Bible study in an apartment complex where a number of church members lived. Bible and notebook in hand, I picked my way through the tricycles and toy trucks strewn along the sidewalk toward my car. It was then I recognized a young man, a Christian, who attended another church, coming toward me like an arrow. He was scowling.

Almost before I could greet him, he lashed out. "You people think you're such good Christians—but you don't practice what you preach! Your own leaders don't live up to their promises." As he continued, loudly, I picked up that there was a problem with the complex managers, Ed and Jeannie, who were members of our church, and something about a promise to have carpets cleaned on a certain day. Evidently the cleaners hadn't shown up.

My heart was torn between politely sympathizing and defending the manager (which would have amounted to defending our church, and Pete and myself). Instead, I was immediately aware of the Bible in my hand.

Almost before thinking, I put my hand up to stop the young man's angry tirade. Quickly, I flipped the Bible open to Matthew 18 and read Jesus' directive to him. I closed the cover again, saying,

"Did you go to Ed and Jeannie about this problem?"

"What good would it do?" he shot back. "They know what they promised. They just don't care what our—"

Again my hand shot up. "You're a Christian, too." (I could hardly believe what sudden confidence relying on the Scriptures gave me!) "I don't want to hear any more about this until you've talked to them. If they won't listen, then come back to me and I'll go with you."

For a couple of weeks I second-guessed my response to the man. I continued to pray for the man and for Ed and Jeannie. But for all I knew, he could be bad-mouthing Pete and me and our church all over the neighborhood.

It was Jeannie who finally mentioned that one of their tenants had come to them in a huff about uncleaned carpets. Ed apologized, explaining that the carpet cleaners had canceled at the last minute and that he had made several unsuccessful attempts to let the man know the cleaning was being rescheduled.

"What amazed us," said Jeannie with a puzzled look, "is that the guy apologized to us for his attitude—as if he had done something wrong. I can't tell you how seldom that happens when you're managing an apartment complex!"

Of course, I told her about my encounter on the sidewalk.

What I want to point out is something I realized later. Turning the angry tenant back to Ed and

Jeannie in no way let me off the hook in terms of Christian responsibility.

In the first place, when wronged people come wanting us to side with them against another person, *we* are wrong to try to help sort things out to see who's guilty. That, as I mentioned before, is entering into the process of assigning blame. To underscore a point I've already touched on, Paul tells us that we are called by God to "the ministry of reconciliation" (2 Cor. 5:18). When we send an angry person off to reconcile with a brother or sister, our responsibility is to pray that hearts will soften and that Satan will not steal into the situation to score a victory by keeping the two parties divided.

Secondly, we must be willing to go with that wronged brother if the offender does become hardened and resists correction. And that kind of commitment cannot be entered into lightly.

When we become third-party to a conflict between two Christians, there is at least one big pitfall to watch out for: We are often quick to take up the offense of another. Let me explain with an illustration.

After a church service, a man in our congregation, whom I'll call Alec, noticed a woman he knew sitting alone in a pew. Casually, he remarked, "Alone again, huh?"

Several days later, the woman's husband, whom we'll call Martin, approached Alec and angrily accused him of offending his wife. Alec had no idea what Martin was talking about. Fortunately, another man overheard the confrontation and intervened. "You shouldn't be coming to Alec with this offense," he said gently. "If your wife was offended, she should come."

This may seem like drawing too-fine lines at first. But jumping in to take up the offense of another usually only causes unnecessary complications. The Bible again and again points us to open, honest communication one with another, relying on other counselors and witnesses only when we can't find resolution between ourselves.

In the case I have just described, an interesting problem revealed itself when Martin's wife was called in. It was learned that Martin had a habit of leaving his wife alone in social gatherings. She tended to be a wallflower, who drifted to the outside of a group while Martin happily chatted with others. It seemed that her underlying motive in mentioning Alec's "offensive" remark to Martin was an attempt to get him to correct his own behavior and stop abandoning her in crowds where she felt insecure. Because she was a non-confrontive person, it was easier to take an indirect approach, saying how much Alec's remark hurt, rather than to say honestly and directly, "You left me alone again, Martin, and it made me feel left out."

As we can see, human communications and relationships are complicated enough between two individuals. Picking up an offense as a third party usually only adds fuel to a fire—and it may be the wrong fire besides!

Another aspect of the commitment we make as a third party is this: Often, people need someone to reinforce good intentions when their own commitment becomes weak. For many of us, we *know* the right thing to do—the problem is in getting ourselves to do it. To have a brother or sister behind us, reminding us of our need to set a relationship right, is sometimes necessary. This can be true not only for those who are terrified of conflict but for those whose idea of settling a dispute is to charge in with guns blazing. In both cases, we can enter into the ministry of reconciliation.

So far, we've talked about taking the initiative when we've been wronged. But what about when we are the offending party?

Jesus said, "If a brother has aught [something, anything] against you," then "go and be reconciled." In fact, He made it clear that we should take this action before trying to go on in our relationship with God. (See Matt. 5:23–24.)

At least this directive is clear-cut when we know that we are truly and solely at fault. This can be as simple as apologizing to your family for being a grouch, not because they did anything wrong, but because you were in a bad mood. Or it can involve going to the business partner you edged out of a good deal. In both cases, there should be *repentance* along with the apology, which means a change of disposition in the first instance and perhaps making financial compensation in the second. Usually, however, relationship problems are not that cut-and-dried. Many times we do or say hurtful things in response to a behavior that we find irritating, or just plain provoking. Maybe you find yourself exploding at the friend who always comments on your children's need for more discipline. What are we to do then?

I believe that the first step is simply to recognize your own sin and be willing to change. Too many times we handle our sin by saying something like this: "I'm sorry I got mad at you, but you really blew it when you said . . ." This approach is really only a thinly disguised way of trying to "save face." It's dodging your own sinful actions and will most likely put your brother on the defensive before the issue of your sin has been clearly dealt with.

Sometimes we're concerned that confessing our own sin will leave the other person thinking he was without fault and that everything is now fine. First of all, it's my experience and observation that when we take responsibility for our own sin, others are usually stirred to take responsibility for theirs. Second, once you've settled up the account of your own offense, I believe it is perfectly fine to raise unresolved issues. Remember though, it is not your responsibility to force someone else to repent and ask forgiveness; just present the facts from your viewpoint.

Maybe all this seems like a lot of work, needing a great deal of emotional energy. I want to give you one final bit of encouraging news.

Most of the rubbings and irritations in our relationships are caused by simple misunderstanding. People often say the wrong thing, then wish they could kick themselves later. Many people, like me, hate confrontation, or they've been trained to avoid sticky issues. Others are blind to some side of their nature and can't figure out why they're always getting people mad at them.

In short, Jesus' directive "go to your brother" is so simple yet so revolutionary. Few of us naturally take that approach. But our Savior, of course, knew the best way to clean out the wounds we receive and the wounds we cause. He knew that most of us are fearful or inhibited or just poor communicators. And He also knew that there is a deep desire in the nature of most men and women to live at peace with others. This cannot happen, in a fallen world with its irritations, unless we are willing to go to our brother.

Once we have risked building new bridges of communication with each other, we are then ready for one of the most powerful experiences friends can share. I'm talking about the life-changing experience of giving and receiving forgiveness.

CHAPTER THREE

"THE TIE THAT BINDS"

P reparing your heart before going to settle a difference is only half the battle. When we made biblical relationships a high priority in our church, we discovered that heart attitude can be a lingering problem. Besides a verbal reconciliation, we need to develop an attitude of forgiveness that permeates our relationship *after* the reconciliation.

The problem for many of us is that seeking and offering forgiveness is not easy. Memories haunt us like ghosts. We know that God forgives and forgets. As David says in Ps. 103:12, "As far as the east is from the west, so far has he removed our transgressions from us" (NIV). And God closes the gap between heaven and earth by binding us to himself with the ties of His love (v. 11). His love never fails.

The question is: How do we bind together our relationships with a godly, forgiving love?

Some time before our church focused on relationships, I wrestled with this question myself. For me, there was one relationship in which shadows of the past had lingered for years. And the embarrassing thing was that the person involved was my own brother. We were both adults, living many miles apart, and were frequently in touch by phone and letter.

One letter, however, seemed impossible to write. I fought to get each word onto the slip of stationery.

"Dear Dave," the letter began, "there's something I should have made right between us long ago. Will you forgive me for all the tension between us while we were growing up? I'm sure most of it was my fault, since I was older and you were just a little child. I was hurt. But you couldn't help it that you displaced me as the baby of the family. . . ."

There. The worst of it was finally out. I breathed a deep sigh and continued, trying to condense years of feeling into a few short lines.

As a little girl, I'd awaited the birth of our new baby with great excitement. The day Dad told my older brother and sister and me that Mom had delivered a baby brother—David—I ran from house to house delightedly spreading the good news to our neighbors.

My thrill was short-lived, though. In no time, that tiny bundle in Mom's arms was stealing away most of her precious time and attention, which had previously been spent on me.

Four or five years later, when I was twelve, my jealousy deepened. Mom and Dad relied on me for weekly baby-sitting while they chaperoned our church's Friday night youth meetings. There was little more than the usual annoyances. David would toddle up to the TV and switch it off right in the middle of a favorite program. Then he'd run shrieking with laughter through the house, with me hot on his heels. For him, it was a game. For me, the whole business was a nuisance. So was David.

After we'd grown up, our relationship remained one of tolerance. No great upheavals. We loved each other. We talked. Our childish rivalry of the past seemed so trivial once I was through with schooling and married to Pete. But there remained the sense of an invisible wall I couldn't break through.

I feel it's important to tell you that there were even very special times between us. Like the New Year's Eve when I stayed home from our Watch Night Service with a cold and Dave stopped by unexpectedly.

He'd gotten off at 11:30 from his shift at a local dairy where he earned money for his college tuition. David's dropping in was not unusual, since the church Pete was pastoring was only fifteen miles away. He'd come by several times to do laundry and stay for dinner. Seeing my "baby brother" was always a pleasure, even though the old, unnameable tension remained, hidden inside me.

But this New Year's Eve visit was very special. Dave obviously loved the Lord, and as we talked, he opened his heart and told me about his longing to serve God full time. Two opportunities for summer service had presented themselves, one with Teen Challenge and one with a dynamic international ministry called Youth With A Mission. Dave's deep concern to do only what Christ wanted impressed me and warmed my heart toward him. Dave had really matured.

Talk about Dave's options went round and round until the sound of Pete's car in the driveway startled us. We'd been at it for several hours! Though it was nearly 2 A.M., we both felt refreshed. It seemed I finally had a friend in this brother.

And yet . . . Why did the nagging feeling *still* trouble me, even years later as I penned my heartfelt confession to Dave? By then, he was interning for a summer with a missionary and stationed on an island in the mid-Pacific, living in a small hut that he shared with a strange little roommate—a rat. It was to this "address" that I sent the letter.

Weeks went by. Would Dave think I was silly? Would my confession rouse hurt feelings in him? Anxiously, I began to check the mailbox daily.

One day, an envelope with a strange postmark awaited me. Dave said a lot in that letter. But the most important words, to me, were these: "I forgave you years ago. I love you."

It is impossible to describe the sense of lightness that took hold of me as I read those words. It was like dropping a forty-five-pound pack from your back when you didn't realize you'd been carrying it. It was like helium balloons being turned loose on a breeze.

Though I've taken some pages to relate this experience, I do so because I think it has important earmarks for us to examine. How does this story apply to you?

Too many of us hold on to the wrong belief that time and distance and silence can eventually heal all hurts. Maybe we don't want to seem petty or oversensitive. Maybe it's pride. Perhaps it's a fear of facing honest emotions. Whatever the case, time is not on our side when forgiveness is needed.

Let's have a closer look at an important scriptural principle from a passage we only touched on in the previous chapter:

> "Be ye angry, and sin not: *let not the sun go down on your wrath*" (Eph. 4:26, KJV, emphasis added).

This directive is linked to the next verse:

> "*Neither give place to the devil*" (v. 27, emphasis added).

The fact is, the more time we allow to pass between a wrong and the moment we ask for forgiveness, the harder it becomes to go to the one we wronged. With the passing of time, our mind makes up more and more excuses to let the offense slide ("I'm sure he's forgotten by now, so why bring up the past"). Not only that, but the passing of time also allows our hearts to grow cold and hard ("I was having a bad day, after all, and he should have seen I was upset in the first place—so he really deserved what he got").

The Apostle Paul warns us to guard against this hardness at the beginning of the Ephesians passage. He says, in effect, "Christ never taught you to act this way!" (Eph. 4:20). And if we are not behaving in accordance with Jesus' principles, then we are giving "place to the devil."

At the end of the passage, you can almost hear Paul's pleading when he writes:

> "Be ye kind to one another, *tenderhearted, forgiving one another*" (v. 32a, emphasis added).

Paul is saying, "Keep your hearts tender by keeping a constant, open attitude of forgiveness." When we refuse to keep our hearts soft toward one another, then, the Bible says, Satan can gain a powerful foothold in our souls.

Now, a great deal has been written about the fact that when you won't forgive, you damage your own health and emotions in the long run. Sometimes we quote James 5:15, which directs us to call for the elders to anoint and pray for the sick. But James 5:16 gets at an underlying cause of many sicknesses when it says, "Confess your faults one to another, and pray for one another that ye may be healed." Harboring unforgiveness can lead to emotionally fed illnesses and disorders.

Much has also been written about the fact that unforgiveness leaves us open to two means by which Satan can continue to defeat us: deceit and accusation. (See Rev. 12:9–10.) It's true that we carry unforgiveness like an invisible scar on our spirit. We may believe the lie that all is well, but Satan can use an unforgiving attitude to poison our relationship with God and others.

It's not my purpose in this book, however, to add much more to either of those subjects. I'm focusing on the effects of living according to biblical principles, because they are there in God's Word. It may be, in fact, that we in the twentieth century have overemphasized the psychological and physiological effects of unforgiveness. It's really very egocentric, when you think about it, to say, "The reason you should forgive is because it's better for your health."

The primary reason we are to forgive is found at the very end of that Ephesians passage:

> ". . . forgiving one another, *even as God, for Christ's sake, hath forgiven you*" (v. 32b, emphasis added).

Good emotional and physical health may indeed be a *by-product* of our obedience to scriptural principles. But the foundational principle is that we forgive others *because we owe to God a debt of love*. God has forgiven us, and we are to freely forgive each other. (For further study on this principle, read Matt. 18:21–35, which is Jesus' parable of the Unmerciful Servant.) Our Master and King asks us to forgive, and when we do, it's this obedience that keeps our heart soft toward Him.

For me, the effect of receiving forgiveness from my brother David did release me from that strange sense that a wall existed between us. I had emotional freedom around him that I had never experienced, even in our best times together. And I have little doubt that the "wall" would have simply disappeared on its own one day.

Even more, the effect that this inner freedom had on my life opened the way to a deeper understanding of what it means to *offer* forgiveness to someone who comes to admit their sin. I found, however, that acting out forgiveness was a lesson more difficult to learn. I wish I could have learned it under easier circumstances.

Marie was a timid young woman, not yet twenty, who often came to our church's youth center. All through high school, Marie and her sister were not allowed to participate in sports or even to attend sports activities. Their parents insisted that they come straight home after school. As far as we could tell, the youth center was the only place they were allowed to go that was not under their parents' watchful protection.

When Marie's parents moved to another state, the girls were given a choice: move with them, or take an apartment together. It was a first breath of freedom—and one that Marie wasn't at all prepared to handle. The girls opted for the apartment, but the sister moved away shortly thereafter. Totally on her own for the first time, never having faced the world alone, Marie was a disaster waiting to happen.

And disaster was what I suspected the day Marie asked to talk to me "alone." Now she was seated before me, fretfully working her hands in her lap. Her long blond hair hung down, nearly veiling her face as she stared at the floor. Then she looked up, tears streaming down to her chin.

"I'm pregnant, Mrs. Caruso," she blurted. "I can't turn to my parents for help. When I told them, my father tried to kill the guy. Now I'm on my own. I don't know what to do."

I tried to think of something to say—something comforting. What kept me tongue-tied, in part, was a vivid memory that played in my head. While Marie sat waiting for me to speak, my mind jumped back several years to another young woman in the same situation.

That young woman had grown up in our church, had baby-sat for our three children. When I learned she was pregnant out of wedlock, I was disappointed, judgmental. My biggest concern was that her sisters not think that we, the leaders of the church, condoned what she'd done.

Several months into her pregnancy, that young woman miscarried. I assumed she was relieved, and visited her in the hospital. Her eyes looked a little glazed, which I took for embarrassment. I said something to her like, "Remember that what you do from now on will have a real influence on your younger sisters."

Only later did I learn that what I'd mistaken for embarrassment was really grief over her loss. Suddenly, I was the one who felt like a fool. Nervously, I waited for her to gain strength and return to church where I could make an apology for my words and cold reaction to her.

She never did return. In fact, I saw her only once, but that was in public and she was with

friends. I never had the chance to ask her forgiveness.

Marie's nervous cough brought me back to
the present. She was still working her hands. This
time, I had to handle the situation differently—
but how?

We prayed together, asking God to give us
both guidance. Then I asked her to come back to
see me in a couple of days. I knew I had a lot
more praying to do. That night I lay awake in bed
long after the lights were turned out. Pete and I
had discussed the situation, of course. Yet I knew
that, because of my past failure, the next move
was up to me. Pete had prayed that God would
speak to my heart, and would be with me all the
way in whatever I was led to do.

I prayed, "I don't want to blow it again, Lord.
Forgive me for my self-righteous attitude. Help
me to love Marie as you do. Let me be a channel
of your love and forgiveness to her."

Still in an attitude of prayer, I wondered how
I could be a channel of His love, what I could do
beyond offering words of comfort. God had
given me so much love. What could I give to
Marie?

A home! The words bolted into my head out
of the air. No, not into my head. Into my heart.

I struggled with conflicting thoughts as I lay
there: *What will the other young people in the church
think? What will their parents think? Will it seem that
we're condoning sin?*

And what about our children? Debbie's thirteen.

What kind of impression will this make on her? How can I expose our children by having an unmarried, pregnant teenager come to live under our own roof? We've been so careful, such a good, straight Christian family . . .

That last thought stuck in my brain—*so careful . . . such a good Christian family.* What was I saying?

The next morning, I checked my impressions with Pete. What did he think about allowing Marie to move into our guest room until after the baby was born? He did not hesitate a moment. We contacted her that day, and shortly she moved in with us.

At this point, I need to break off the narrative to point out some of the things this experience taught us about forgiveness as a family and as a church.

A lot was revealed in my prayer. I'd asked God to forgive me of my self-righteousness, not fully aware just how deep that attitude was ingrained.

The first lesson we learned had to do with uncovering a sinful *self-concern.* In my case, it was a concern about our reputation as leaders in the church and a concern for what the "good" kids would think.

On one occasion, when the Pharisees belittled Jesus for associating with sinners, He replied, "It is not the healthy who need a doctor, but the sick. Go and learn what this means: 'I desire mercy, not sacrifice' " (Matt. 9:12–13).

It became clear to us all, in the months that our church family responded to Marie's needs, that we are most often concerned about the needs of the "healthy," while we are unconcerned or are afraid to involve ourselves with the needs of the "sick." Let's face it, we all want smooth, comfortable, trouble-free lives.

I'm not saying that you should open your home to every troubled person who comes along. But I am saying that you must recognize self-righteousness when it clogs your heart. And that you must open your heart to what God's Spirit would have you do if you want your life to conform to His living Word.

This leads to the second major lesson we learned about true forgiveness.

In the same passage in Matt. 9:9–13, we find that the Pharisees were right about Jesus—He did associate with Publicans and sinners. He ate in their homes, laughed with them and listened to their troubles.

Many of us, on the other hand, place a big distance—emotionally and sometimes literally—between ourselves and a person who is in need of forgiveness. This distance communicates the attitude: "You have to come up here to my level. Then you can be forgiven." I have no doubt that is what I communicated to the young woman about whose influence on her younger sisters I was so worried.

This is not the kind of attitude God has shown toward us. In Rom. 5:8 we read: "God demonstrates his own love for us in this: While we were still sinners, Christ died for us." In a real sense, God *accepted* the task of bearing the eternal penalty of our sin, and He continues to *accept* the task of walking through the result of our sin, right at our side.

This, then, is the kind of acceptance we must be willing to demonstrate if we are to offer forgiveness fully—a willingness to *accept*, in part, the burden of the one who is in the wrong. What does this mean, practically speaking?

Each of us has certain areas in which we're weak, certain ways that we always seem to "blow it." It may be gossip that hurts or slanders, it may be sexual temptation, a problem with alcohol, tobacco, drugs, or it may be an uncontrollable temper. How much easier it is to overcome those sins and drives when we have the support of other Christians who accept us while we are on the road to "cleaning up our act." You, by demonstrating the kind of acceptance that we learned, can show the face of Christ to a weak brother or sister who is beset by sin and longing for freedom and healing.

To finish Marie's story, our church learned how to help shoulder the burden of her pregnancy with her. Women were helpful in their counsel about her health. Marie continued to find fellowship among her peers as she continued to participate in youth activities, including a short drama the group put on.

As to my fears about the influence on my children, those anxieties could not have been more unfounded. Many evenings, the children would pass by the living room where Marie and I spent many hours talking. Sometimes the kids would see Marie sobbing in my arms. Now that they're older, they tell us they never for a moment thought it would be "okay" to end up in Marie's position, regardless of the love that was shown.

On the night of Marie's labor I was at her side. After the birth of her baby, Pete and I and many others stood by her as she went through with the crucial decision she'd made earlier about the child's future. She had chosen to give up her baby for adoption, a very difficult and emotional decision for her to make.

Today, Marie is a happily married wife and mother. Through her prayers and forgiving attitude, both of her parents have become Christians.

True, this is just one story and it happens to have a very happy ending. Sometimes the transformations take longer. Some "miracles" are slow in coming. But developing a heart that is both soft toward God *and* willing to show His forgiveness by sharing in the healing of others opens the way to forming relationships on a much deeper level. I'm talking about the joy of living *transparently* with one another.

Transparency is a term frequently used among Christians these days. By transparency we generally mean the ability to be open and honest with each other, to share our opinions, deep thoughts and hurts, no matter how large or petty they may seem. It's the opposite of covering things over with a false kind of politeness for the sake of keeping relationships smooth and bumpless; also the opposite of living in "nice" but isolated relationships in which we really don't know each other very well at all.

To be sure, open and honest relationships are a high goal and one for which we should be working. They bring health to us as individuals and health to the body of Christ as we learn to be open in the oneness of Christ's love. (See John 13 and 14.)

The problem, in my experience, is that several foundational principles of Scripture need to be in place first before we can achieve transparency and unity with each other. Going to your brother to "make up" or "get things right," and forgiveness and acceptance are only part of building godly relationships. For us and for our church, they were among our first lessons.

Yet some Christians act as if these principles are the only ones in the Bible. We frequently hear people say, "If only we would stop looking at each other's flaws and just accept one another, the church would be so much better off."

But that cannot be completely true. Otherwise, God would never have given us other foundational principles on which to build our relationships. He would not have given us instructions on how to handle good and bad reports, or shown us how to love those who are hard to love—those we sometimes refer to as "the tough cases." He would not have given us directives for relationships in the home, between husbands and wives. He would not have spoken to us about building strong relationships in the church—between pastors and flocks, and then between Christians and those in the world who need our light and love.

As one church, we learned that to stop at acceptance leaves one with weak and neurotic relationships, allowing sin to continue and hindering true spiritual growth. We must grow to a place where we are willing to confront in love. By this I mean a willingness to confront both deep-seated attitudes in ourselves and sins and wounds in the lives of others. These go hand in hand, and they are steps that will lead us to a deeper maturity as Christians *on the way to transparency*.

It's to this process of deeper maturity that we must look now.

CHAPTER FOUR

"WAIT TILL YOU HEAR THIS"

Many times, we as Christians become privy to important and even intimate information about others. It's ingrained in the nature of our Bible studies, Sunday schools, prayer groups, and even our friendships to ask for prayer and counsel from one another. Too often, however, our "sharing" crosses over an invisible line and becomes damaging, without our intending it.

The Apostle Paul exhorts us to focus our conversation only on things that are true, honest, just, pure, lovely, and things that are of "good report" (Phil. 4:8, KJV). Another expression used here is: "whatever is admirable" (NIV).

Obviously, there are times and situations that require us to talk about "people problems" that are not admirable or of good report. What are the guidelines that can help us when these situations occur?

Our struggle to learn these guidelines—as a

church and as a pastoral couple—happened under some of the most difficult of circumstances.

Doug and Barbara Andersen were among several of our church families who lived in the same apartment complex. This was the complex in which we held a women's Bible study, the study I was leaving the day I met the man who was angry about his uncleaned carpets. Even the managers, Jeannie and Ed, belonged to our church. A wonderful warmth and closeness developed between the families who lived here, including the Andersens.

Then came the near-tragic incident that made me question whether this closeness would prove to be such a good thing after all. Through this incident, however, we learned a great deal about handling vital and very personal information about others that we have become privy to. Or, to put it another way, we learned the difference between gossiping and giving good reports.

Barbara Andersen was a lovely blond woman, her hair always styled nicely to complement her blue eyes and high cheekbones. Not long after I met her, Barbara confided that her careful attention to personal grooming and dress was, in part, her way to compensate for another characteristic one noticed right away.

Barbara walked with a decided limp. It was the result of a childhood accident that left one leg shorter than the other. Those closer to her may have also detected a limping in her spirit as well. As a child, she had been teased by other children, and she confided to me that, as a result, she often felt conspicuous and uncomfortable in groups as a result.

I felt compassion for Barbara. My first thought when she came to mind was not, "She's the woman who limps." I thought of Doug, her husband, who was a Christian and seemed to love her very much, and of Wendy, their pert eight-year-old. Though I could sense Barbara's reluctance in groups, I did not pick up the deep, deep wounds in her spirit. Nor were any of us aware that Barbara was facing one of her worst fears.

Then Pete and I received the shocking phone call about Barbara's suicide attempt.

Doug and Wendy had been out working in the garage and had gone in to find Barbara lying across her bed, her head dangling off at an odd angle. Beside her lay the tranquilizer bottle she had emptied. Doug sent Wendy running to call Jeannie and Ed. Paramedics had rushed Barbara to a hospital, but they had no way of knowing if she would make it.

That night, Pete and I stayed with Doug and Wendy in the waiting area outside the emergency room. We prayed, and tried to comfort Wendy. Near dawn, we were notified that Barbara was going to live. The doctors made it clear that she would need a long time of quiet and rest in order to recover physically and emotionally. Pete and I invited Doug to move his family in with us, at least for a few days, so we could support and counsel them at close range.

After Barbara was released from the hospital, however, I wondered if we had made the right decision.

First of all, it was clear that Barbara was in a dangerous state emotionally. She and I spent long hours talking, curled up on our living room sofa, and a painful story emerged.

Doug and Wendy were close and they enjoyed each other's company very much. On one hand, that made Barbara happy. But it also struck another chord deep inside, down where there was a crack in her self-esteem. At times when she saw them doing things together, a voice in her head taunted her, "They really don't need you. In fact, maybe there's someone who would be better for them."

She'd been able to fight these thoughts for years—until she learned Doug's terrible secret: He was having an affair. Worst of all, he was seeing a model, a perfect beauty, the image of everything Barbara felt she was not. For several months, she fought for Doug's affection, trying to be cheery and loving. But the affair continued.

Doug's rejection hit like an earthquake, opening the fissure that Barbara had fought to keep closed. It even seemed to her that Wendy preferred her dad. Self-loathing and self-pity burned through all Barbara's resistance. And so, one evening when Doug and Wendy went out to work in the garage, Barbara reached for her prescription tranquilizers.

As she looked at me now from across the sofa, I was chilled to think of the promise she'd made the day the hospital released her: *I'll do it again if I get a chance.*

Barbara's emotional state and spiritual needs were just the first problem. The second major problem complicated things even more. Pete and I sensed the need for complete confidentiality in this situation. Could she face the church, knowing that *they* knew? How would Barbara gain ground on her already poor self-esteem if gossip about her attempted suicide should spread? What if she bumped into one of those chatty and full-of-advice-in-the-middle-of-the-grocery-store types? It might even trigger another attempt.

In fact, Barbara and Doug's story has an intriguing ending to it. It's with their blessing and approval, of course, that it's repeated here in the hope that it will benefit others. We'll look at what happened in this *particular* instance shortly. For now, let's examine some biblical principles that can guide us in handling good and bad reports about others.

The United States government has coined a term that refers to the passing along of important and even secret information. Individuals are selectively chosen to receive information on what is called a "need-to-know" basis. One of the first guidelines we can use when it comes to handling privileged or delicate information is to share our knowledge only with those who need to know.

Immediately the question arises: Wouldn't that include anyone who knows—let's say, the Andersens—and might be called on to fast and/or pray for them?

The answer is no.

Why not?

It's time we were honest with ourselves and admit that sometimes we "share" information because it lets others know that we are "in-the-know." Instinctively, many of us sense that knowledge equals power and position. To be "in" on privileged information makes us feel important. Who among us can resist when someone pulls us aside and whispers, "What I'm going to tell you now is strictly confidential . . ."?

If we want to build relationships on strong and true biblical principles, we're going to have to truly examine our motives when we give or receive information about each other. Very simply, we must ask ourselves, "Does this person *really* need to know?" Or, "Do I really need to be in on this?"

Of course there are very definite occasions and positive reasons for divulging private or possibly damaging information. And there are ways that it can be done effectively so that the results are constructive, not destructive.

First, let's consider who might be *included* in the "need-to-know" category. You will have to make a decision in a given situation based on these recommended guidelines.

We found with the Andersens, and with numerous other varied situations over the years, that a simple rule applied. Those who need to know are persons who are either *part of the problem* or *part of the solution*.

In the Andersens' case, that immediately excluded a large part of the church, even though they might have been counted on for prayer support. It did include only those responsible for overseeing Barbara and Doug's spiritual support. In this instance, Pete held the pivotal position in counseling and standing by Doug.

Now let's suppose a friend has come to you for help with a very personal problem. Your "need-to-know" list might include a Sunday-school teacher, Bible study leader, or the close Christian friend of the one who is struggling. Be clear on this: We're not referring to *your* teacher, group leader, or close friend. We can inadvertently spread reports about others by going to outsiders for advice. It would have been a violation of the Andersens' trust and confidence for me to have picked up the phone and called someone who had no direct influence in the crisis, and spill their story.

Only those who are directly related to the persons involved should be called in at first. Why? Because they are the ones whom God has already chosen to have a role in your friend's life.

If you think that your friend might benefit from talking to another Christian or to a professional counselor—someone who has either personal experience or counseling expertise with the same problem—consider this as a good guideline: Ask your friend's permission to share the information, or introduce your friend to the counselor. Then step into a position of prayer and emotional support—and seal your lips.

Once you've determined that a person fits into the "need-to-know" category, here are some further guidelines. Remember, in trying to follow the biblical patterns, our goal is to keep the report a good one. What does this mean?

It means that you share only as much detail as the person you're involving really needs to know. It is important *not* to add your own judgments. ("He's such a terrible husband—I've never known him to live up to his word"; "She's the most controlling woman I've ever met—it's no wonder he's run off with his secretary.") Your judgments can be prejudicial, coloring the way another will view the problem. In fact, your perspective is only that—your perspective. Though you think so, you may not have all the facts. Your goal is not to get the third party to agree with you, but something higher. What is that goal?

The goal, which we so often lose sight of in "counseling" relationships, is that of helping the hurting person to remove the blockages of sin and emotional damage so that they can move on in their relationship to the Lord. We are talking about encouraging someone on to maturity—no matter what we think their "fault" or "sin" might be. We are not out to prove how sharp our insight or wisdom is.

This rule applies even if we are talking about the most ordinary situations. In fact, it's in the ordinary events that most of our relationship problems take root.

For instance, let's suppose you're on the planning committee for a church holiday open-house, which is aimed at welcoming new people from the community. You need a hostess for the function, someone who can be at the church an hour before the event to take care of last-minute touches. Someone suggests Betsy, but you know that Betsy is rarely on time. You pick her up each week for a Bible study and often wait forty minutes while she applies her makeup, feeds the cat and ... well, you get the picture.

Now, the others on your committee don't need all the facts about Betsy's tardiness. (I've been in many such meetings—and even in large-group settings—where someone felt they had to "share" all the details. In the past I was probably guilty of it myself.) Nor will Betsy benefit from your poring over her faults while you smirk and roll your eyes. You can simply say, "I don't think she's the best choice for that function," and leave it at that.

At the same time, as discussed in Chapter 2, it may well be your obligation to go to Betsy and let her know that her tardiness causes a problem. But don't cause further problems for her by giving her a bad reputation among others without giving her the opportunity to see her fault and take steps to change.

Most important, examine this directive from the Apostle Paul. It's familiar, but too often unheeded:

> Love does not delight in evil but rejoices with the truth. It always protects, always trusts, always hopes, always perseveres. (1 Cor. 13:6–7, NIV)

Another version puts it this way:

> If you love someone, you will be loyal to him
> no matter what the cost. You will always be-
> lieve in him, always expect the best of him,
> and always stand your ground in defending
> him. (v. 7, TLB)

Can you honestly say that is your attitude
when you have "news" about someone? Or when
someone wants to share an interesting tidbit of
news about a friend? We need to be reminded—
all of us, over and over—when dealing with the
reputations of others to live by Paul's admonish-
ment: "Let love be your highest aim" (1 Cor. 14:
1).

To put it simply, passing along bad reports
about friends and acquaintances without following scriptural guidelines can be destructive for
them. And it can be embarrassing for you.

Recently, I became aware of this true story,
in which any of us could fit our names. (These
names have been changed at the request of the
people involved.)

A friend of mine, whom I'll call Cary, was
stopped in a shopping center one day by Jim, a
Christian friend who was an elder in "Bible
Church," a fellowship across town. To Cary's sur-
prise, Jim began to tell him about "problems" at
Bible Church involving the pastor and the pastor's wife. Because Jim was a friend, Cary listened.

"Most of the elders are about to resign and
walk out," Jim told him. "We think Pastor Jones

is into false doctrine. Besides that, his wife is too controlling. She wants to control everyone's personal life. Bible Church is turning into a cult. We're getting out."

A few weeks later, Bible Church *did* split. For months after, Cary and his wife picked up more and more tidbits about the Joneses, all incriminating, from other friends who had left Bible Church. Some of the stories were shocking, because Cary and his wife had been friends with the Joneses, but had been out of touch for some time. They *assumed* their friends had gone off the "deep end"—though they did notice that sometimes the negative stories conflicted. By then, the Bible-Church split had affected the whole community, and many long-time Christian friends were no longer speaking to one another.

Still, when others asked Cary what he knew about the Bible-Church split, he innocently passed along the stories he'd heard.

But was he really innocent?

Two years after the split, Cary and his wife felt led to leave their own small church for a larger one. It was a clean break, no hard feelings between anyone. But when Cary prayed for direction as to a new church home, he did not receive guidance from the Holy Spirit, but conviction.

Cary felt the conviction that he had believed bad reports about the Joneses *without ever going to them to see if the reports were well-founded*. The Holy Spirit seemed to be telling him that he had sinned. Whether the reports were true or not wasn't the issue, Cary had forsaken his Christian obligation of love to these friends by not checking with them about what he'd heard. If the accusations were true, he might have confronted them in Christian love. If the stories were false . . . well, that was suddenly painful to consider, because he'd passed them along to others as if they were gospel.

Cary felt that before the Lord would give him further guidance on a church home, he needed to go and ask the Joneses' forgiveness. (It also occurred to Cary that all the stories had come from those who left Bible Church, and none from those who had stayed. Those who'd stayed were strangely quiet in the face of the accusations.)

Cary made many interesting discoveries when he visited the Joneses. With great humility, they admitted how they had contributed to the split by becoming defensive when challenged. What had begun as a doctrinal question (that might have been ironed out) intensified into a power struggle between the pastor and his elders. By then, stories were flying fast and wild.

When finally hearing the facts, Cary felt more than satisfied with the Joneses' response to the accusations. In the end, Cary and his wife joined Bible Church. A professional journalist, Cary now says, "I can't believe that, when relating to other Christians, I violated one of the basic rules of my own trade: Don't report hearsay; go to the source."

Maybe we expect other Christians to live up to a standard that's too high. Or maybe we expect them to live up to the *wrong* standard—ours. It may be that you need to take a personal inventory to see whether you're only too willing to believe the bad report, or whether you're following Paul's principle of always believing the best *first*.

These are the guidelines we learned as a church through months of walking a fine line as we tried to help Paul and Barbara Andersen. They helped us learn the difference between giving a "good report"—one that helps a situation and does not diminish the ones involved—and a "bad report"—one that is passed on for selfish or sinful motives and is potentially destructive.

As I mentioned, the Andersens' story had a remarkable conclusion that taught us a final lesson about the reports we make about others.

Pete and Doug spent many, many late nights together, probing the meaning of marriage and examining Doug's feelings about Barbara. He decided, after soul-searching, that he loved Barbara and wanted to try to make a go of it. Shortly afterward, they moved back home to work on their marriage.

Pete and I prayed hard, wondering if they would make it—and wondering if stories had circulated about the Andersens that might get back to them, threatening their chances of success.

Months later, when Barbara rejoined the women's Bible study in the apartment complex, I held my breath. Would someone's remark tip off Barbara that people had been talking behind her back? Such a slip might undo in an instant the ground she'd gained in rebuilding her self-esteem.

During a time of sharing, a newly divorced woman asked for prayer for herself and her sons, that they might be able to adjust to the life of a broken family. There were prayers, then offerings of comfort and hope.

Then Barbara began to offer her support, saying, "I know how hopeless life can seem. Last year when I tried to kill myself, I felt so—"

Her words were cut off by a loud gasp from the dozen or more women seated around the room. Barbara looked stunned. "You mean . . . you didn't know? I thought everyone knew."

A few admitted they thought there had been some problem, since the Andersens had moved in with us for a time. Personally, I was amazed, since only two or three newcomers had joined the group after Barbara's near-tragedy. The rest of us knew each other very well. Could such a shocking event really have been kept quiet by the half-dozen people who had been involved?

I asked how many had really *not* known. Most hands went up, even the hands of women who lived in apartments only a few steps away from the Andersens.

Barbara's eyes glistened with tears. "This surely makes me feel loved. I've felt conspicuous all this time, thinking that everyone knew. Now that I think of it, those of you who *did* know continued to love me. You never treated me any differently."

One woman spoke for all the rest of us: "If something this dramatic could happen right under my nose, and no one gossiped to me about it, I *know* I can trust you all now. I feel so secure."

That, to me, is one of the greatest compliments a group of Christians can receive. For so many come to our churches and study groups, bearing hurts and the cares of the world, looking for a shelter.

One shelter that we can build for them is the careful, loving handling of their secret hurts, which is sometimes translated "counsel"—and other times "prayer and silence."

CHAPTER FIVE

SPEAKING THE TRUTH IN LOVE

One relationship problem that came up again and again in the period when our church focused on renewing relationships was this one: Many times we see in a Christian friend certain behaviors that not only offend others, but are real and dangerous blocks to their own spiritual growth. This is a problem deeper than the occasional, everyday relationship scrapes we discussed in Chapter 2.

In our hearts, we feel an obligation to go to that friend and tell him how his behavior is causing a problem. Many times, though, we back out. We say, "Who am I to talk? I'm not perfect either." Or, "Well, that's just Bob. He's been that way as long as I've known him. He just has a 'blind spot.' " Or, "We have to accept one another, faults and all. After all, Christ accepted me."

I want to point out a crucial distinction between the popular usage of the word *acceptance*, and the biblical usage of the word. In large part, we made the distinction in Chapter 2: Biblical acceptance means a willingness to help "bear one another's burdens," as Paul directs in Gal. 6:2. But that verse is so often quoted out of context by those of us who have huge pools of compassion in our hearts. Paul says, in the previous verse:

> Brothers, if someone is caught in a sin, you who are spiritual should restore him gently. (Gal. 6:1)

The "gently" part should help the compassionate ones among us to accept another of the most important biblical relationship principles. As Paul puts it in another letter, we are called to "speak the truth in love" to one another. (See Eph. 4:15.)

In my experience, this principle seems to give Christians a great deal of trouble. Some feel it gives them the right to pick others apart for anything at any time. Others think: "It really wouldn't be loving to point out someone's flaws or sins, would it? Better not to say anything at all."

It's crucial for us to recognize God's motive for giving us the responsibility in Christian relationships. Eph. 4:15 tells us to love each in this way so that "we will in all things grow up into him who is the Head, that is, Christ."

Our *purpose* in going to correct a brother, then, is not to force him to conform to our standards or opinions, but to help him to grow in maturity in the body of Christ. Our *attitude* in going should be that of a servant, not of someone who has a right to correct because of superior behavior. We are to go because we serve Christ and He tells us to go. Humbly.

Not long after Pete began to emphasize this principle in our church, I heard this account involving two women I'll call Cassie and Jan.

Cassie was visited at home one day by Jan, whose hesitant attitude told Cassie that this was not a casual drop-in. She wondered what was wrong.

Seated on the living room sofa, Jan immediately fell silent. Then she began to weep softly. Cassie was not really prepared for what Jan said at last.

"This is hard for me to tell you, Cassie," she began. "But I feel you need to know. So many times when we're together, you dwell on all the negatives—every bad thing that happens to you, no matter how big or small. Cassie," Jan faltered, "I feel that you do this because you're seeking attention and sympathy."

Cassie was stunned, unaware of any such motive, and immediately became angry. Frozen, barely able to speak, she gave little response. After a long, awkward silence, Jan left.

For days, Cassie endured an internal wrestling match. How could Jan, her *friend*, say something that hurt so deeply? Who was *she* to correct anyone? Yet Cassie knew that it had not been easy for Jan to confront her. She finally asked God to show her if what Jan said was true.

Gradually, in a few days' time, Cassie had her

answer. The Holy Spirit convinced her, by re-minding her of specific instances, that Jan had been absolutely correct—not only in her assess-ment of Cassie's self-pitying and manipulative at-titudes, but in the humble, brokenhearted atti-tude in which she had come. Jan, because of her long-standing love for Cassie, was probably the only person who *could* have confronted her.

Cassie was undone by Jan's love and willing-ness to risk rejection. She wept for a long time in repentance before calling Jan to admit she had been right.

I want to point out an important facet of this account. Jan and Cassie had already established a *commitment* to one another by virtue of their friendship. It was this foundation of love that wore down Cassie's resistance to the unpleasant facts.

In our congregation, we chose to make a def-inite commitment to "speak the truth in love" with an eye toward helping each other see our blind spots. Verbalizing that commitment seemed to unlock our *frozenness* about going to one another and made us more willing to receive correction, too. (We'll talk more about that aspect of it in the following chapter on "transparency.")

Let's face it. It is a risk to go to someone with a word of correction. We risk saying it the wrong way, hurting them and being rejected. That's tough to face! Therefore, I recommend, when possible, to verbalize such a commitment, be-tween Christian friends, to lovingly correct one another when necessary.

One very important caution: Pointing out each other's faults, shortcomings and sins is not something that should be done in a group setting. Some organizations undertake this kind of group confrontation, such as Alcoholics Anonymous and other behavior modification clinics. Those groups, however, are normally supervised by trained professionals. Confronting someone with their flaws in front of even a small group—say, a Bible study—can bring devastating emotional results.

It's important, then, that the setting be private and comfortable. In this way, you can direct a friend's attention to one of his or her blind spots without destroying dignity or self-esteem.

This approach—commitment mixed with a caring atmosphere—is often enough to help a friend let down his defenses and listen to what you have to say. Usually—but not always.

It seems that in every church or fellowship, there is at least one individual who can be referred to as a "tough case." This is the man or woman who rubs you and everyone else the wrong way most of the time. They can't seem to open their mouths or raise an eyebrow without causing a conflict. Somehow it's hard to believe their abrasiveness is unintentional. So most of us tend to avoid these folks. But God wants to help them.

No one changed more, as we learned what it meant to speak the truth in love, than Art. In the first chapter, I related an incident at one of our church picnics when Art gave his five small children a verbal blast for budging off the blanket where he'd ordered them to sit. That was typical of Art. At that time, few of us would have referred to him as a friend.

Art's stocky build and bushy red beard reminded you of a friar. But his mercurial temperament made him act like anything but one. You never knew when you were going to say or do something that would detonate his temper.

The rough side of Art made it very difficult to appreciate his good qualities, which included a precise and brilliant mind and a gift for simplifying complicated procedures or equipment. In fact, as it is with many of us, Art's greatest strengths contributed to his greatest weaknesses.

For instance, he stoically marched up to Pete after one Sunday service to correct him. Though others who had been touched by the sermon were there to ask further questions, Art made his point emphatically: Pete had used the word "continually" several times when he *should* have said "continuously." To Art, the content of Pete's sermon was not as outstanding as his misuse of a word.

When Art was present you usually felt a certain amount of tension. No one knew when the "land mine" would go off.

One time, in particular, a number of church families were camping together, including Art and Penny and their children. Art happened to pass by a group of teenagers involved in a water fight—and got splashed accidentally with a bucket of water. He chased the girl who was responsible, picked her up and carried her to the water faucet to douse her. Trying to escape, she twisted, fell from his grasp, and landed with a thud in the muck beside the faucet.

Art announced, "I don't get mad, I get even." Everyone, the adults who witnessed his outburst as well as the teenagers, stared at him in disbelief.

Things were even more difficult for Penny and the children. At home, Art demanded neatness, order and quiet—apparently without taking into consideration the normal noise and mess five little kids can make. When he arrived home from work, authoritarian rule began: The house was to be shipshape and the children silent. An infraction could set off an explosion. Otherwise, he mostly ignored the children.

As if this were not enough to fray Penny's spirit, he seemed devoid of sensitivity to her needs. The moment he was ready to leave a gathering or church service, Penny had to drop all conversation, no matter how important, and leave immediately.

It wasn't that people had never confronted Art before. He had lost jobs because of relationship problems. His bosses, however, did not take the time to confront him about his behavior. They just let him go.

Several people at church, however, began to feel their obligation to Art—and to Penny—to talk to him about the effects of his temper and personality. One woman, Gloria, tried gently to talk to him about his rough treatment of the teenaged girl on the campout. When Gloria asked him to forgive her for harboring bitterness toward him, he replied offhandedly, "Oh, sure. You're forgiven."

I must make a pause in Art's story at this point to make some brief but important points.

Perhaps there is a "tough case" person in your life. Maybe you, like Gloria, have tried to talk to this person about troublesome behavior, only to get a cold shoulder or even a fiery response. What you may need to do is apply some biblical principles *before* you go to the individual.

Prov. 15:1 says: "A gentle answer turns away wrath, but a harsh word stirs up anger."

Normally, we think of this verse as applying to the following type of scenario: Someone snaps at us, or comes with a hostile spirit, and we are to reply with gentle, Christlike words. But have you ever wondered why this can be so hard to put into practice?

What these wise words are pointing to as well is our need to examine our underlying attitudes—our inner response to another's personality and mannerisms. Much of the time, we have formed inner judgments and reacted inwardly to people before it is necessary to respond to them verbally.

Therefore, when we feel we must go and "speak the truth in love" to someone, we should first spend time in prayer taking a long, hard look at our true feelings. Certainly you want to give a kind, Christian response; that's the goal. But are there other things you'd say to this person if you were not a Christian? Have you had angry, imaginary conversations in which you blow this person out of the water with what you'd *really* like to say?

It's true that your "tough case" person may have sinned against you, or others. But before you go, you must deal with your own sinful reaction to their unruly behavior. You must be able to admit to yourself and God, if it's true, that you are angry, resentful, or bitter toward this person. At this point, it's easy to see how one of Jesus' directives applies:

> How can you say to your brother, "Let me take the speck out of your eye," when all the time there is a plank in your own eye? You hypocrite, first take the plank out of your own eye, and then you will see clearly to remove the speck from your brother's eye. (Matt. 7:4–5)

Inner anger or bitterness, or a self-righteous attitude are among the "planks" that can be buried in us. Too often, we read this verse and give up any thought of confronting someone else in his sin. But God wants us to deal with our inner attitudes, then go. Practically speaking, there is an important reason for this.

If you have not recognized, confessed, and been cleansed of a bad attitude, it's almost certain to come through in your conversation. Rather than *revealing* sin or shortcomings in an attitude of restoration, your voice is likely to take on an accusing tone. And if the person you are speaking to comes back with a cold or angry response, your own reservoir of anger can suddenly shoot up like a geyser—even if you honestly did not intend it to. The encounter can make a bad situation worse.

So often we confuse biblical "transparency" with dumping our emotions. There is no healing or restoration in that approach. But a clean heart is a vital prerequisite for speaking the truth in love.

Let's return to Art's story, because it reveals further insights for dealing with the "tough cases" among us.

Gloria, who had attempted to call Art's attention to the truth about his rough behavior, later told me she had examined her heart before going to him. She confided, "I don't feel that my going helped him to understand how his actions affected us at all. I felt that I was healed and forgiven—but I saw no remorse on his part."

But God was at work in Art's life in another way—one that taught us all great lessons.

Dean, our son-in-law, had developed a friendship with Art. Both men enjoyed hunting, camping, and doses of wilderness solitude. Dean was able to handle Art's "rough edges," and was not interested in changing him. But Debbie, our daughter, had witnessed too much abrasive treatment of Penny and the children and had a hard time liking Art.

When Dean announced the two families were to take a camping trip together, Debbie was not overjoyed. For a week or more before the trip, she prayed that God would prepare her heart, unaware that this was the first step in the start of a miracle transformation.

After several days of observing Art's typical treatment of his family, Debbie decided it was time to speak. She chose a time late in the evening, when all the children were asleep and when Dean and Penny would be there. She knew she needed their support and the stability of their presence.

While the embers of the campfire burned low, Debbie began to speak gently but directly to Art.

She told him how most people felt they had to walk on eggshells around him for fear of his cutting remarks and his temper. She described his treatment of Penny and the kids, giving specific examples of the way they had to jump to his commands and times he acted or sounded as though he didn't care to have them around. "You don't treat them as humans, much less as family," she finished.

Minutes passed, with only the hiss of the campfire to break the silence that hung between them all. Debbie spoke again. "I laid it on pretty thick. Don't you have anything to say?"

Art responded slowly, indefinitely. "I'll have to think about it for a while—a few days. Then I'll know how to respond. To take action or something."

A hidden door in Art's heart opened from that night on. Change did not come instantly, of course. One key, perhaps, was that Debbie called to his attention specific instances and behaviors from an outside viewpoint. This was also reinforced by others, especially Dean.

Once, as they were driving along a mountain road during a hunting trip, Dean said, "Art, I need to tell you how you threaten people with your technical expertise."

"What do you mean?" Art inquired. Dean could tell he had real interest.

"Technical things come easy for you," Dean explained. "When you talk, you assume others are with you, but they're intimidated. Maybe you're not aware, but most people feel intimidated by someone who seems to know more than they do.

"And you know what?" Dean continued. "Sometimes you really do come across as a know-it-all. It's great that you retain everything you read. But you don't always have to express an opinion about every subject that comes up."

Likewise, other men at church began to explain to Art how this know-it-all manner was quite likely his biggest source of trouble on the job. Art later confessed to Penny that he was beginning to see what the men had meant: He had made a suggestion to his boss, only to have it turned down. But when a guy who was a real charmer made the same suggestion, the boss readily accepted it.

In short, Christian brothers and sisters had made a long-term commitment to Art—not to see him change for their benefit but for his own and his family's. The secret was helping Art to make connections between the *intent* behind his actions and words and the actual *effect* he really had on people.

As Art took a long, hard look at himself, he decided to work at changing. He shared more of his previous inner thoughts with us.

Today, Art is a different person. He is still a little rough around the edges, as we all are. But things have changed drastically in relationships—especially with Penny and the children.

The children are no longer afraid of Art, and he continues to work at being a caring father. When he came to recognize his wife as his greatest ally, he began to support her as an individual. In fact, he helped her discover undeveloped potentials supporting her decision to go back to college. Today, he encourages her as she lectures on her favorite subject, astronomy. Together, the family explains to visitors the heavenly wonders they're seeing as they look through Penny's high-powered telescope—a gift from Art!

Art (whom I now call on to give me technical advice about my computer!) has told me he was long aware that he gave out "mixed messages." He knew that he seemed gruff and unapproachable. He just hadn't known how to change that aspect of himself. And when he felt the disapproval or rejection of others, he only closed off from them more and more.

Art's transformation may seem too good to be true, as accounts in books sometimes do. I assure you the changes were not made overnight, and were most surprising to Art himself. One of the main lessons we all learned was that it's easy, in the weakness of our flesh, to bail out of relationships that don't seem to work. God wants us to commit to each other for the long haul.

I must add that, in the long process of Art's transformation, most of us who knew and dealt with him were also changed to some degree. You never can witness the specks being wiped from a brother's eye without having a plank or two drop out of your own! What many of us learned were important steps to more sensitive communication.

I'll close this chapter by summarizing some of the points we learned:

1. You may be carrying wounds or inner anger (even on behalf of another if you are the caring sort), and these need to be dealt with in private with God before you can speak the truth in love. Accusations destroy. The truth heals.

2. The person who annoys others with an ingrained mannerism, or with a repeated offense, may be entirely ignorant of what he is doing. Before going to him, ask yourself if this may be true.

3. If the person is aware of the problem, he or she may not know how to change. Your commitment to be a faithful brother or sister in Christ to the person can give the needed encouragement and love to stick with the changing process.

4. Go as a learner, not as one determined to set the other person straight. If you cannot affirm the person honestly when you go, you are not ready. Go back to prayer. (Caution: Don't use this as a dodge! Sometimes God will tell you to go in faith.)

5. Be prepared to readjust your understanding of the situation according to the other person's perspective. You may be surprised at what you learn about your reactions—positive and negative—from that other person.

6. When speaking, give specific examples of a person's problem, not generalizations. (Say, "Yesterday, you interrupted six people at the Bible study," not, "You talk too much.")

7. Expect defensiveness. It's a mechanism we all use to defend ourselves. Gently, patiently, keep the conversation open.

8. If it seems too much for the other person to accept at the moment, don't be a know-it-all. ("Well, you just pray about this. I know God will show you that what I'm saying is true.") Retreat until God shows you it's time for another conversation.

9. Close the conversation with prayer and with affirmations of friendship and commitment.

A final word. Once you are willing to enter into this kind of relationship, with one other person or in a group, a beautiful thing begins to happen. You begin to help build eternal values and characteristics in each other's lives. You are being used by God to help one another conform to the image of Christ.

This kind of commitment makes possible an atmosphere in which we lay down our own defenses and fear of risk-taking. Then we discover the wonder of transparency.

CHAPTER SIX

TRANSPARENCY

At several points thus far, we have lightly touched on the subject of *transparency*. One Scripture passage that offers wisdom regarding godly relationships was written by John, known as the Apostle of Love:

> God is light, in him there is no darkness at all. If we claim to have fellowship with him and walk in the darkness, we lie and do not live by the truth. But if we walk in the light, as he is in the light, we have fellowship with one another, and the blood of Jesus, his son, purifies us from all sin. (1 John 1:5–7)

Transparency, or "walking in the light," is a worthy goal in our Christian relationships. For many of us, friendships can be superficial—even when we think we are being open. I know from experience.

When Pete began to teach on transparency in our church, I didn't listen too closely. I thought that, if anything, I was transparent and honest. Was I surprised!

I recall quite vividly one morning during this

time. It had been an especially hectic week, and I was way behind in my housework. That morning, Pete was all set to drive the children to school. He was already outside, revving the engine when our son, Mike, came charging out of his room. "Mom, I can't find any clean socks," he pleaded. "And Dad's waiting!"

"I'm sorry," I replied, "but I haven't had a chance to do the laundry. You'll have to retrieve some from the hamper." Reluctantly, Mike rifled through the hamper, then charged out to the car.

Later that morning, I was visiting with a friend, a woman at whose home we were planning a baby shower for one of the young women in our church. Offhandedly, I mentioned my wild morning. "I even had to send Mike off to school wearing dirty socks."

"What?" my friend responded. Her jaw dropped open. "You mean that happens to you, too? Why, Bev, I thought you were always on top of things. I never see your house dirty. Your kids' hair is always neat. I can't believe it."

On one hand, her reaction to my confession about the socks was a compliment. Or was it?

My friend rushed on, "You know, I'm not a very good housekeeper. The laundry is always overflowing the basket. I'm always behind in dusting. I used to try to live up to your example, but I decided I couldn't do it. So I gave up trying."

I had to chuckle. And I painted for her a more accurate picture, something like this: Many were the times I'd heard a car pull into our driveway and I panicked. In the seconds it took for the visitor to park, step out of the car and get to the front door, I would have run from the kitchen through the living room, desperately snatching up out-of-place items with one hand and swiping at dusty surfaces with the other. Then I'd rocket down the hallway, pitching my armload of things one by one into the appropriate rooms, slamming each door behind.

By then the doorbell would ring. On my return flight, I'd swoop by the bathroom to tear a comb through my hair. In a moment, I'd be opening the front door with my "Well-what-a-surprise!" smile in place.

Had I presented my life as so neat and efficiently run, in an effort to be a good model for other Christian women, that I'd become little more than a glossy snapshot? A false picture of perfection? My friend's response that morning made me take a long, hard look at my idea of transparency.

Once I began to wrestle with questions about my own ability to be open and honest, I was suddenly aware of the struggles of others with these same questions. I found myself intensely interested in learning about this area of transparency.

What I saw immediately was that, as with any other goal, you have to grow into transparency. It also requires some preliminary steps. One of them is to weed out false notions of what we mean by the term.

Perhaps the most common error we make is to think of transparency as emotional dumping.

This can happen in a couple of ways.

The first is to spill your feelings to others about some wrong they've done or some good they've failed to do. Some Christians, misinterpreting transparency, feel they're at liberty to dump raw emotions *whenever* and *wherever* the mood strikes. But if this is done without preparing your heart in prayer, and without preparing the feelings of the recipient, about the only thing that is accomplished is resentment on his part. You might feel better for having unloaded, when actually you've only dumped the heavy burden on unsuspecting shoulders.

Another kind of emotional dumping happens frequently in our "prayer and share" groups. Let's face it, many of us long for intimacy with a friend or a small group of friends with whom we can be ourselves—whether we're having a good day or a bad one, whether we're spiritually up or scraping bottom. The thing we need to be careful in gauging is whether the kind of "sharing" we do in a given setting is really *appropriate*.

A friend recently told me this story, which illustrates the point.

Jerry and his wife are involved in a Bible study group made up of members of their church, meeting one night a week in the home of the group leader. Not long ago, a young wife and mother, whom we'll call Luci, began coming to their group. At her first opportunity, Luci began to pour out intimate details about her husband's drinking problem, her undisciplined children, and some emotional upsets of her own. The group prayed for her, and during the week two of the women spent time with her.

The second week Luci came, the same thing happened, and again the third week. Each time, the group prayed for Luci briefly, and then went ahead with a study. Again, Luci's obvious plea for help was followed up by one of the women. But shortly, Luci became frustrated and even openly critical. Finally, just before she dropped out of the group, she said angrily, "This group isn't very warm. I won't be coming back."

According to Jerry, everyone felt bad and a little confused. Were they really cold and indifferent? Why had they been unable to help her?

Looking back, Jerry says, they now see that there was a big gulf between the established purpose of the group and Luci's expectation. Everyone but Luci wanted primarily to study the Bible. Because of her deep and real needs, Luci needed counsel. But realistically, there was no one in the group who felt qualified or comfortable in counseling her. Many, in fact, were brand-new Christians themselves, who didn't have much wisdom to offer her.

Luci nearly left the church entirely, Jerry says, until one of the women from the study group took time to gently point out the expectation problem. The woman explained that Luci perhaps needed the *friendship* of those in the group, which they truly wanted to give—but not necessarily their in-depth counsel. Then the woman offered to help Luci find a wise Christian counselor. Together, they did find one who helped Luci deal with her husband's drinking and the discipline of her children.

Now Luci has returned to the Bible study group. When personal needs are shared, she freely asks for prayer. She's formed close, supportive relationships that extend outside the group.

The point is, that most often we can do each other a favor by defining the limits of a relationship. We should *always* be ready to offer Christian love and prayers, but we're not always called to counsel. One of those preliminary steps on the way to true transparency—in the deep, life-changing sense—is to begin with an atmosphere of *commitment*.

Ken, a close friend of ours, recently expressed his experiences with transparency in a group of men who were committed to one another. He made some important observations, which deserve recounting:

I've often seen deeply personal things shared in believers' gatherings. Then someone may follow up by mentioning a scripture, or giving a general exhortation—and then the meeting moves on until it closes in prayer.

Our group recognized the failure to pray specifically for an individual's shared needs. So we agreed never to discuss a personal need or victory in a meeting without addressing it in prayer. We discovered that this helped each man to see himself as a minister in the body, and watched as each one began to grow in his own area of spiritual gifts as he prayed.

When it came to sharing areas of personal struggle, I found that I would typically begin describing the symptoms in a rather objective manner—almost as though I were speaking of someone else. I found that this kind of sharing, which was common among us, inevitably brought a "moment of truth."

The other men would have to decide whether I was dealing with the real, deeper issue, and whether I was facing up to it. Once they confronted me with their observations, I had to decide if I was ready to deal with the root problem. When I was ready to open up, then the others could draw out my feelings and minister to my hurt or exhort me to take action based on biblical principles.

With this kind of transparency—in a setting of love and support—you may find that for years you've had mostly a head knowledge of the Bible. Now, suddenly, you have the chance for real spiritual growth that surpasses anything you've imagined.

The kind of atmosphere Ken describes can be developed not only in a regular group setting but by Christians who live or work in close proximity. We saw it happen in our church among a number of families who lived very closely together. The story of one man, we'll call Fred, is witness to the transformation a commitment to transparency can make in the life of someone struggling to overcome a weakness.

Fred had a problem with his temper, and he knew it. One moment he would be discussing Scripture, and a moment later he might fly into a rage if someone disagreed with or upset him. He was like a time bomb, ready to detonate if you made a wrong move.

Fred's temper brought other stresses into his life. His marriage became a battleground because his wife, Denise, added fuel to Fred's always-smoldering fire by her responses to him. At work, he was liked and known as a good employee, but one day his boss told him flatly, "Fred, we'd promote you—but we can't trust you. You're too volatile. We never know when you'll blow up."

Because of his temper, Fred knew his life was in danger of running out of control. More than anything, he wanted to be respected as a man and as a Christian. But with every outburst, he seemed to be further and further from reaching that desire.

Fred had made a commitment to Christ, and he truly wanted to change. Now he made a commitment to allow other Christians to confront him. He and Denise lived in close proximity to several other Christian couples, and he gave them permission to walk closely with him through the problem, confronting him when necessary about his angry outbursts. He knew he couldn't go to church on Sunday and smile at everyone as though nothing were wrong if they'd heard him shouting at Denise on Saturday night.

Interestingly, most of the people involved

shared the conviction that Fred didn't need to be confronted about his outbursts. Rather, it was when he separated himself and sulked about his weakness that he was roundly confronted. And this is the way it was done: He was firmly but lovingly reminded of his commitment—and affirmed that he was truly loved, that others wanted to be near him. They demonstrated respect for him through their acceptance, encouragement, and constant love.

One of the most touching examples of that loving respect came from Ed, his best friend.

On a sunny summer afternoon, some men from the church took their boys to the beach to fly kites. During a playful wrestling match, Fred lost his cool and began to get rough. Ed wrestled him to the sand and held him there until he agreed to stop fighting. When Fred got up, he grabbed his son by the arm and stomped off in anger.

Frustrated, miserable with himself, Fred went home and crawled into bed. After all, he didn't even like himself. So how could he expect anyone else to like him? He just wanted to sleep and forget it all.

But a couple of hours later, he was awakened by the touch of a hand on his back. Kneeling beside the bed in prayer was Ed.

Fred knew then what a deeply loving and firm commitment this was—a commitment that could not be shaken. In this way, God's love and concern for him was demonstrated by Christian friends who would not just "accept" his temper, but were willing to stand beside him regardless of his behavior. He learned that he could "blow it" and still be loved.

As the awareness of others' love for him grew, we witnessed a gradual but marvelous change in Fred. It seemed that once the pressure to perform like a "perfect" Christian was lifted, so was a large amount of his frustrated anger. Through that acceptance, and with the prayers of those who were committed to him, Fred was eventually freed from the tyranny of his own temper.

Today, Fred has learned to truly like himself. Through committed, transparent relationships, he was made to see that a deep lack of self-respect had fueled and refueled his anger. So great is the change in Fred that he's been promoted six times, moving from a laborer to project manager of a large company!

Fred says now, "Without the support of my Christian friends, I wouldn't have been able to sustain my marriage or my Christian walk during those years of anger."

Judging from these experiences, the reason it is so vital to learn transparency—or to "walk in the light," as John puts it—is that we are so often blind to the *real* roots of our problems and sins. At best, we deal with surface symptoms most of the time.

This has been true since the Garden of Eden. When Adam and Eve sinned and broke their perfect communion with God, the first thing they did was try to hide and cover themselves.

When God called out and asked why they were hiding, Adam replied, "I was afraid, because I was naked" (Gen. 3:10). But Adam and Eve's embarrassment because of nakedness was only a *symptom*. At the root lay disobedience and rebellion—followed by the desire to cover up and protect themselves from God who, in the words of the Apostle John, *is light*.

It wasn't that Adam and Eve were really afraid of being seen naked. They were terrified that God's light would reveal their sin. They hoped He would look only on their outward appearance and leave the inner sin of rebellion untouched.

But God will not do that. And so He has given us others in the body of Christ to help with the necessary process of bringing truth to light.

When you give others permission to help you see yourself in the light, and when they lovingly accept that obligation, true transformation can come. Then the character of Jesus Christ can be more radiantly revealed through your life.

I want to add a personal comment because of the conscious effort it took me to change years of habit and old ways of thinking. Among them was the attitude that a leader (or his wife) should be a "sterling" example and not show any weaknesses.

As I began to reveal my true self to others, I tended to go to extremes. Sometimes I spilled everything, and was probably a little obnoxious and monopolizing. (It's so easy to go on and on when you've got someone's attention, isn't it?)

Gradually, I've learned that transparency cannot be forced on others; it can only be offered. It's an attitude, a willingness to be open and genuine for the sake of personal change. It can also be offered as a way of helping others to open up and face attitudes and sins that are buried in their lives. From there we begin true, spiritual ministry to one another. Learning to be transparent has opened my eyes to the wonder of being a part of the body of Christ.

Once we allowed this kind of openness in our relationships, it helped us to apply biblical principles in another truly important area of our lives. For many of us, the most painful battles—and the greatest rewards—were yet to come. For we were just learning how to apply these principles in the place where it is the most difficult of all to behave as a Christian—in our own homes.

CHAPTER SEVEN

SPIRITUAL HEADSHIP

As we mature in relationships with other Christians, one of the most vital concepts we need to learn is the place and power of spiritual headship.

If a Christian man, for instance, does not understand this concept, his life is likely to be like a ride on a rocky road. He may pay only lip service to authority, never truly trusting his spiritual growth and direction to a pastor. He is likely to hold on to a hidden pocket of reserve, an "escape hatch," the sense that he can always bolt out of any relationship that starts to make him accountable for his actions. And whether or not he ever becomes a husband and father, he is likely to mishandle authority when given a leadership role.

A Christian woman who does not understand spiritual headship may find herself on a continuous emotional and spiritual seesaw. On one hand, she may struggle to "submit," trying to wipe out her own sense of guidance, her God-given intelligence and personality. Or she may seize the headship from her Christian leaders—be it husband or pastor—because she believes she is "more spiritual" than they are.

Whether or not you are single or married, a leader or a potential leader, a balanced view of spiritual headship is needed.

One of God's most beautiful illustrations of spiritual headship was painted on the fabric of everyday life. It is a godly relationship between a husband and wife. The Apostle Paul had the Spirit-inspired insight to see God's masterwork when he wrote:

> The husband is the head of the wife as Christ
> is the head of the church, his body, of which
> he is the Savior. (Eph. 5:23)

Today, thanks to the Holy Spirit's guidance through wise teachers, we are seeing a restoration of godly marriages and lines of spiritual authority in the home. By examining transformed marriages—especially the transformation of a husband into a godly leader—we will more easily understand the importance of spiritual headship.

I'll never forget the morning our marriage, and our understanding of Pete's role as a godly man, was changed forever. It wasn't one of those "Cinderella" moments, accompanied by the sweet singing of bluebirds. In fact, it was rather painful for both of us.

Pete had invited a visiting missionary to speak at our church one Sunday morning. Ron's wife joined him on the platform. After Ron brought a message from God's Word, he and

Ruth moved among the congregation, praying for various needs. From my seat near the side of the sanctuary, I could see the cleansing tears and the joy-filled smiles on the faces of those the Millers touched that morning. It was an uplifting time for everyone.

After the service, we drove Ron and Ruth to a nearby restaurant for lunch. I remember thinking how beautifully this couple worked and ministered together—what great oneness I sensed between them. And I recall the little twinge of longing I felt.

For years, I'd wanted to be an integral part of Pete's ministry—not just a background figure or a resource. Not that I didn't carry many responsibilities, but I wanted to be closer to Pete and his work. I wanted to be at his side, ministering to people with him. So far, it hadn't happened. I hoped that during our lunch, I could slip in some questions about the husband-wife relationship—gently, of course.

At the restaurant, our new friends told story after story of their work in Argentina. They spoke with such enthusiasm and brightness. And at the central core of everything they shared was the warmth and closeness of their relationship.

I must admit, I was feeling a little envious. Then Pete surprised me with an abrupt declaration. In a moment's lull, Pete said, "Ron, I'm jealous of the way your wife ministers with you."

Ron very patiently explained that he made Ruth's spirituality a priority. He said he knew how easy it was for a Christian man to be so caught up in his business, whatever it may be, that he unwittingly neglects his spiritual responsibility to his wife. He said that he and Ruth made daily concerted prayer together a top priority. He finished with a strong pitch to Pete about putting a spiritual relationship with me at the top of his list, followed closely by the governing of our household.

I'm embarrassed to say that my inner response to what Ron said—especially the part about praying together—was, "That will be the day!"

Not that Pete wasn't a man of prayer. In Bible college, he had started a 6 A.M. prayer meeting. Over the years, he'd met with various other ministers for early morning prayer. And we had what I called our "good-night prayer" together, which was sort of a wrap-up prayer for the day.

But, what I longed for was a deep unity in prayer, a spiritual relationship in which we prayed in agreement about the common problems of life in our active household. I'd been trying to get Pete to pray like that with me for years with no success. Long ago, I'd given up trying.

After lunch, I wondered if Ron's suggestion about praying together had made any impression on Pete. I certainly never expected he would take it as a mandate from God!

The next morning, Pete informed me that we were going to start praying together every day—starting right then. As we knelt together, I was overwhelmed with his impassioned confession of having neglected the spiritual aspect of our relationship. And the following Sunday, he continued to amaze me when he made this announcement to the congregation: "For years, I've made myself available to everyone else. My wife has even had to make appointments with me just to talk about household needs.

"Now I see that Bev is my number one 'sheep.' And I intend to minister to her needs first."

Even for those who are not married, the number-one key for taking on the role of spiritual headship is *commitment*.

The first thing Pete did was to commit to a regular time to pray and read Scripture together. For us, the best time was first thing in the morning. I realize that this may not work for everyone, since the workday starts very early for some and getting children up and off to school can also compete. The point is to do what works for you— and most of all to make the commitment. Setting a regular time, whenever it may be, will help you to keep that commitment.

For husbands and wives who want to build this kind of spiritual fellowship into their marriage, I urge you to find the format that works for you. A devotional book can be helpful, as long as it does not become an end in itself. I suggest simple, honest prayers. This may not be easy at first. But the rewards in renewed, open communication are wonderful.

I also recommend making a commitment to read the Scriptures together. It does not have to be a long passage. You might take turns reading short passages aloud. Very quickly, you will find yourselves drawn into discussions about God's Word, and you will find it easier to think about a given passage all through the day. And as you think about it over and over, it will gradually work its way into the center of your life.

Pete and I began praying together by taking turns. Soon we found that when one of us prayed about something, the other often sensed that God had already answered the prayer, or would have an insight into the situation being prayed about.

Gradually, we moved into a method of praying that became almost a three-way conversation. If one of us was praying, the other was free to insert a brief comment, much the way we do in casual conversations with others. Sometimes the Lord would bring things to our minds that would lead us in an entirely different direction from the things we'd set out to pray about.

The most important thing, of course, was the work that God was doing in Pete's life. Because this chapter is focused toward men, I've asked him to share insights that he has gained in the years since his understanding of spiritual headship became clearer:

Like most men, I suppose, I thought success had nothing to do with the home. A man's sense of self-worth generally comes from successes outside the home, mainly from his job. The world measures a man's success by whether or not he rises to the top in his field, by the amount of money he earns, and by the admiration he receives from numbers of people.

God created men with the desire to succeed, and there is nothing wrong with these feelings. But unless a man is taught where true success lies, he has no understanding of his responsibilities first to God and, if he is married, at home. He thinks of his roles as husband and father primarily in terms of the paycheck he brings home. And his mind dwells on his job, quotas, deadlines and promotions.

Even ministers tend to view their position in this light. Our work is the ministry. We counsel, teach, and meet people's needs. We tend to think we're successful if we can do these things well, if our congregation is growing, and if the church's programs are operating smoothly. As a result, we are just as likely as other men to neglect personal spiritual responsibilities and the needs of our families.

But the Bible measures success differently. The foundation of success has nothing to do with money, not even with family and friends. True achievement, by the biblical standard, is found not so much in what we do as in who we are. The more we become like Jesus, the more truly successful we are. The deeper we develop our relationship with the Creator, the greater our prosperity.

The notions we have of success from a human point of view tend to focus on the outworking of this relationship with God. The man who loves God will obviously be taken care of by Him. The man who communicates with God will understand how to manage his life wisely. The one who loves God will love others. It is easy to see why the only occurrence of the word *success* in the Bible describes the effects of obedience to the Word of God (Josh. 1:8, KJV).

We too often accept the world's definitions of success as our goal.

I did the things I thought would make me a success. I now see that those were things that satisfied my ego. I became a workaholic, though I didn't see it that way. I thought I was "sold out" to God. I didn't know how to take time to enjoy my children, and even felt guilty if I took a half day off to visit my mother.

I also knew Bev had been wanting me to pray regularly with her. But I could not see the importance of it, and I was blind to this need in her.

When Ron told me I should pray with Bev every day, I received it as a charge from God. I was able to see, gradually, that I had been thinking the way the world thinks, not God's way.

For instance, consider God's view of Abraham. God considered Abraham a success and vowed to show him all that He was going to do. Why? God said, "For I know him, that he will command his children and his household after him, and they shall keep the way of the Lord, to do justice and judgment" (Gen. 18:19). God did not evaluate Abraham according to his wealth or popularity, but by the way he fulfilled his office of husband and father. His "household" was also his business. Inasmuch as he was faithful in these areas, God blessed him.

Through my prayer time with Bev, I learned that God views the home as a small unit of the church. He places each married man in the office of husband, and sees every man as a minister in his own home. For those of us called to service in the church, the Apostle Paul gave a prerequisite in the form of a question: "How can a man who does not understand how to manage his own family have responsibility for the church of God?" (1 Tim. 3:5, The Jerusalem Bible).

I also came to a better understanding of Bev through our prayer time. I realized that God created women to receive their sense of success and fulfillment in a far different way than men. A wife's desire is "toward her husband" (Gen. 3:16). I saw that Bev, like all other women, is happiest when she knows that her husband truly loves her and is committed to showing he cares for her.

Learning how to meet Bev's needs came through reading the Word and through my relationships with other Christian men. Primarily, of course, it came as we shared our lives at a deeper level.

As I built my closest relationships on biblical principles, I realized the need for other men to be taught in this area.

Most Christian men are surprised to learn that it is their God-given responsibility to see that their children are well taught. We can certainly delegate portions of that teaching to teachers, but we cannot blame the church or the public school system if our children do not grow up in the wisdom and knowledge of God, or the character that He wants in their lives.

With these goals in mind, we must stop viewing our success in worldly terms. With God's help, we can become true "heads" of our families—that is, the chief example of what it is to be a Christian. With His help, we will become the husbands and fathers God intended us to be.

No passage of Scripture is more central to understanding what it means to be a godly man than Ephesians 5. Let's look at what that role entails.

Earlier, we looked briefly at Eph. 5:23. It is important and bears a second look.

He has headship. "For the husband is the head of the wife, even as Christ is the head of the church, his body, of which he is the Savior."

In the natural world, we hold the head of a corporation or the head of a government responsible for all within that organization. Just so God holds the husband responsible for the condition of the marriage and the family. Jesus is the example of the husband's headship. We are to lead our families in the same loving way that Jesus leads the church. That means that a man cannot sit by as a spectator, passively observing his wife as she carries the weight of household responsibilities. Nor can we be dictators, laying down the law. We are to serve as administrators, actively involved in the family life.

He loves. "Husbands, love your wives, even as

Christ also loved the church and gave himself up for her" (Eph. 5:25a).

Jesus' love for us was self-sacrificing even to the point of death. As a husband, I am to give myself sacrificially for my wife, not looking out for what I can get from the marriage, but seeing to her needs and interests. Naturally, we desire to look out for our own comforts, but if I truly love my wife I will set those needs aside for her. That means that I will look to see whether she needs help with the children—even if I come home tired from work. Or I will stop and listen if she needs to talk—even if it means turning off the ballgame on television.

He sanctifies and cleanses. ". . . that [Christ] might sanctify and cleanse [the church] with the washing of water by the word" (Eph. 5:26b, KJV).

A husband must view his relationship with his wife as *sanctified*, which means "set aside for a holy purpose." Just as the Word of God encourages, corrects, exhorts and builds up the church, so should the words of the husband wash and cleanse the spirit of the wife. That means putting an end to criticism, complaining, sarcasm or ridicule. If a husband tells his wife she is lazy, clumsy and a hindrance to him, she will live up to his words. But if he tells her she is needed, appreciated and lovely, she will become radiant.

He presents her to himself. ". . . to present her to himself as a radiant church, without stain or wrinkle or any blemish, but holy and blameless" (Eph. 5:27).

Just as Christ is preparing His bride, the

church, for himself, a husband can help mold his wife into the woman she was meant to be. As I've already implied, the husband's attitude has a strong influence on the atmosphere of the home. He can either help his wife to grow spiritually, or he can cause her to feel beaten down and depressed.

A pastor friend once told me that he can discern what kind of husband a man is by looking at the countenance of his wife. Perhaps that is too flat a statement, but I think there are times when a woman's face will reflect her husband's care for her—or the lack of it.

He loves his wife as his own body. "In this same way, husbands ought to love their wives as their own bodies. He who loves his wife loves himself" (Eph. 5:28).

Most men take pride in the way their bodies are cared for. They are concerned about exercise, nourishment and rest. A loving husband will see that the wife's needs in these areas are taken care of as well. He will notice if she is fatigued and run-down, and will be sure that she takes good care of herself. Too many men behave as though their wives were their mothers, expecting them to be a source of constant nourishment, support and clean socks. If you fall into this category, start turning the picture around by learning how to care for your wife's needs.

He will nourish and cherish her. "For no man ever yet hated his own flesh; but nourisheth and cherisheth it" (Eph. 5:29, KJV).

A Christian husband will suggest areas of

reading or times of relaxation and refreshment that will renew his wife's spirit. He will cherish her by protecting her from attacks by relatives, outsiders, from complaints or dishonoring remarks by the children, and from self-lacerating comments and attitudes she might harbor.

He leaves his father and mother. "For we are members of his body. 'For this reason a man will leave his father and mother and be united to his wife, and the two will become one flesh.' This is a profound mystery—but I am talking about Christ and the church" (Eph. 5:30–32).

Just as we, the spiritual church, are part of Christ's body, so the wife is part of her husband. A Christian husband will recognize the need to establish his own family as separate and distinct from his parents and in-laws. He will take up his responsibilities, develop his relationship with Christ, and look to his own parents and his wife's as advisors who have more experience, though they are no longer the "heads" of his family.

There is another scripture that I find central to understanding the husband's role in the marriage relationship. It comes from the Apostle Peter. "Likewise, ye husbands, dwell with [your wives] according to knowledge, giving honor unto the weaker vessel, and as being heirs together of the grace of life; that your prayers be not hindered" (1 Pet. 3:7, KJV).

You can see from the scriptures already cited that God is very concerned with the way we treat our wives. If our relationship with them is poor,

He warns us that our prayers are likely to be frustrated or cut off.

How can a husband live with his wife "according to knowledge"? By recognizing that she is his equal before God, a joint heir of all God's blessings. He will also study his wife, getting to know her through observation and dialogue, asking her to help him understand her innermost thoughts and feelings. He will pay attention to what she says, and to her expressions and body language.

Let me say a final word about the scriptural principles we've been looking at. All of this can seem overwhelming, and there are two mistakes that are easily made.

One is to say, "It seems impossible to measure up to the things Pete is talking about." With that attitude, you'll give up before you start. Or you can set out today to change yourself overnight and find yourself complaining at your wife tomorrow. Then you might say, "Well, I've blown it. I'll never change. I might as well go back to being the old me." No one ever climbed Mount Everest without conquering many, many smaller peaks first. Don't give up if you set out with God's help to change.

But *do* set out! The riches you will find in loving your wife as Christ would have you love her are worth every moment of prayer and effort. If you have not already begun to build your marriage relationship on these principles, begin today. If you've been at it awhile, keep up the good work. There are more rewards ahead.

As Pete taught about the principles of spiritual headship, there was a dramatic change in the men of our church. Not only were they becoming more dynamic Christian husbands and fathers, they took on a gentle yet definite authority as leaders. We saw more solid commitments to the work of the church.

As might be expected, this change among the men was paralleled by a change in the women of the church. As we gained a biblical perspective on the role of men, it was amazing to watch how the women began to blossom and move into their God-appointed roles.

I would be misleading you to leave the impression that this happened overnight and was easy. For many women, understanding our place in submission to our "spiritual heads" was difficult at first. A majority struggled to find a new sense of identity. We had questions about our need for fulfillment as a person. Did "submitting" mean giving up our personhood?

I must admit that I, the pastor's wife, seemed to struggle with these questions most of all.

CHAPTER EIGHT

WHAT IS SUBMISSION?

It was a comment I wished I hadn't overheard.

Pete was talking with a group of people after church one Sunday when I heard him say proudly, "Bev and I have been married all these years and we still have not had an argument."

Every time I heard him make that statement, my stomach knotted. Perhaps I'd been holding in some irritation. I don't recall. But I thought, *Of course we haven't had any arguments. I never disagree with you!*

Believe it or not, my inward admission that day turned on a light inside me. It was the first time I'd dared to admit, even to myself, that I was less and less comfortable with the concept of submission. Or at least what I thought of as submission.

I was not quite eighteen when I became Pete's bride. How deeply I wanted to be a perfect, submissive wife, just like Ephesians 5 said I should be. The best model of a godly marriage that I had seen while growing up was my grandparents, Grandma had never disagreed with Grandpa on anything, at least not in my hearing. I assumed they had a perfect marriage. I'd thought, as a young bride, that I would be just as happy and content as Grandma if I let Pete make all the decisions and if I never spoke my mind and just worked at being a submissive wife.

And that's what I did, to the best of my ability, for quite a long time. Now here I was after all these years of marriage and three children with a lot of pent-up frustration. Pete's comment about having had no arguments triggered a landslide of inner reactions. Who was I? What did I think about any given issue? I'd agreed with Pete so long I didn't even know if I had any opinions that differed from his. "Surely this can't be what God had in mind for me," I concluded.

Suddenly I was faced with a challenging thought that, I now realize, had been dawning for some time: Did I really know what submission meant? Or was I missing out on true fulfillment in marriage?

When I began to ask other women their thoughts on the subject of submission, I found a broad range of opinion. Several who had non-Christian husbands said they felt they should be submitted to them only in certain things, and a couple said they didn't have to submit to their husbands at all. After all, these women said, they had the "mind of Christ" and their husbands didn't.

Among those who had Christian husbands, the response also varied. Some took what is commonly called the "doormat" position in which they didn't express an opinion on anything. Others submitted only in certain areas where their husband made a "big deal" of a given topic. More than a few shrugged and said they had fairly smooth, "normal" marriages and submission had never been an issue.

"We both submit to each other, I guess," one woman told me brightly. "He vacuums for me when I need help, and I let him have time to go hunting with his buddies. It all evens out."

I want to say here that none of the notions mentioned describes the most healthy marriage relationship. A strong marriage is one in which each partner is growing in love for the other, growing toward his/her full potential as a human being, and growing in love and service to God.

After years of studying many translations and versions of the Bible, I have discovered several principles that give a more accurate understanding of submission. They have changed my idea of marriage—very much for the better. And they've opened up broader possibilities for understanding such a potentially confusing topic.

Eph. 5:22 says, "Wives, submit to your husbands as to the Lord." One translation uses the phrase, "be subject to your husbands." At first, I could not get a handle on this. Then an idea came.

I thought of a good friend of mine, a woman whose husband is an alcoholic. In many ways, her life was sadly "subject" to his, because she never knew when he would come home drunk. But then a more positive example came to mind. Since Pete was a "pioneer pastor," setting up new churches at that time, he made a very small income. In a very real sense, my life was subject to Pete's then. Not only that, but he could be boisterously outgoing, embarrassing me in public places with his loud "hallelujah!" He was also a spur-of-the-moment person and he liked spicy food. These characteristics in Pete were unchangeable.

Then I discovered another rendering of Eph. 5:22, which said that wives should "adapt" to their husbands.

Let me say that, as in the case of my friend with the alcoholic husband, I do not think a wife "adapts" to alcoholic behavior by accepting her husband's drinking. Today, there are good organizations and good counselors from which a wife—or a husband—can seek help when a spouse is alcoholic. A husband or wife will need to adapt his or her own behavior, in response to the alcoholism, in order to help the spouse to change. By that I mean they will have to be willing to attend counseling or even intervene by calling together friends and family to confront the abuser, opening the way to treatment and healing.

Problem relationships aside, I could easily see how the word *adapt* must apply to the role of a wife.

For instance, I could envision myself as a garment, nicely made and intended for my husband. At first, the garment did not quite fit Pete's build.

I'd quickly learned that altering Pete was not an option. He was the way he was—not bad, but I could not expect him to change. In these areas, the "garment" was altered to accommodate the build.

From this small metaphor, I understood that when a woman becomes a wife, she does not need to lose her identity or personhood. But as she (the garment) willingly alters herself to "fit" her husband, he looks better—and so does the garment! One accentuates and brings attention to the attractiveness of the other.

Even though I'd considered myself a submissive wife, this picture opened my eyes to the ways I subtly tried to alter Pete to fit me. Women can have great influence by the little comments they make. I found myself praying, "Lord, forgive me for trying to remake Pete the way I'd like to see him. Help me to pray for him in his weaknesses, and to encourage him in his strengths."

All this laid a good foundation for my new understanding of the wife's role in a marriage, at least on one side. The wife is to be the encourager and supporter of the husband, not his critic. But big questions remained: What about the wife's identity as an individual child before God? When God looks at a husband and wife, do the two of them just blur together in His sight, so that a woman and her own desires are no longer visible?

The first scripture we turn to in answering these questions is Proverbs 31, with its wonderful picture of the godly woman. Some women bridle when the Proverbs 31 woman is mentioned. They feel this woman, if she really existed, was some sort of over-achiever who makes the rest of us look bad. I can't view the Bible through such a negative lens.

To me, the Proverbs 31 woman is a liberator. She is proof to me that God says all things are possible *for every woman as well as for every man.* (See Luke 1:37, my emphasis added.) She can serve God in the home, in business, in ministry, even as a man can.

Then how do we tie this verse together with the instruction in Ephesians to be submissive?

Real clarity on this point came when I heard Betty Coble, a pastor's wife, speak on this subject (she is widowed).

Betty intrigued me when she compared a wife's submission to her husband with applying for a building permit. Her metaphor was ingenious. It was also one that I could relate to because we had just built our first church building with our own hands. And I had gone with Pete to the building department so many times that I had the procedure down pat!

When you are building, you must submit clear blueprints to the proper authorities in your locale. After an allotted time period, you receive their decision. They may say that your plans are approved, disapproved, or they may ask you to make recommended changes and resubmit the plans. Most of the time, you're asked to make recommended changes. This may be for safety or health reasons, because certain architectural styles are required in a given area, or for any number of good reasons. The changes are rec-ommended, not to destroy your plans, *but in order that your plans will fit in well with a larger picture.*

This analogy still sends a warmth of excite-ment through me! It means, first of all, that I can have plans that originate in my own heart and spirit. It means that God wants me to use my own gifts, strengths, talents, and to achieve His dreams for me. But my husband still holds the God-given responsibility for being the shepherd of the household. So I cannot run off and do things without his knowledge, counsel and ap-proval. I must submit myself to my husband.

That means God wants me to submit all that I am to Pete—my ideas, fears, intuitions, opin-ions, plans. Once I submit them to him I am to wait, just like at the building department, until he decides what to do with them.

Again, I can feel the fears and frustrations of many women who would ask, "What if he says no to something I want to do—or to something I feel God wants me to do?" I, too, used to struggle with Pete's rejection of some of my plans and ideas. I had always felt it was my place as a godly wife to keep silent and not complain. That was tough!

But, returning to our metaphor, a building department can deny your permit—and you still have the right of *appeal.* This happened to us in trying to build our church. The application was denied by a clerk; Pete appealed to the depart-ment supervisor, and the decision was reversed.

In a marriage, a wife can and should appeal

to her husband if she feels he is making an unwise decision. It is not biblical to let your husband make all the decisions without your counsel. Some women take the position that it's "safe" to operate in this fashion—because then they are not responsible for blunders! This is a self-centered, self-protecting position that needs to be shed. It is an immature position to take because it does not allow for growth in maturity. Others feel that the husband is *supposed* to make all the decisions, but, again, the Bible does not support that view.

In Gen. 2:18, we read that when God created Eve, she was to be a "helpmeet" to Adam. That did not mean that she was created just to wash his socks. (He didn't have any!) It meant that she was to be a vital completion to her husband. And we women today are to be the completion of our husbands as well. What does this mean?

In God's wisdom, He saw to it that there should be a masculine and a feminine perspective on things. We need both these viewpoints. A husband who makes decisions concerning the family finances, for example, without considering what it will do to the wife's household budget for food, clothing and school expenses is basing his decision on too narrow a view of the situation.

As I mentioned earlier, we women do have the power of influence with our husbands. It's a position of power that is sacred before God. It can be wasted on complaining and manipulation, which is clearly a wrong use, or it can be used wisely.

There also may be times a wife believes her husband is acting on a wrong decision even after she has appealed to him. Then, as at the building department, she can appeal to a higher level. She can go with boldness to the throne of God and ask Him to deal with her husband. God may change her husband's heart, or He may let him make a mistake, or He may assure her husband that his decision was right in the first place.

Many fear that by relinquishing the ultimate, decision-making power to their husbands, they will be treated as less than equals. Their dilemma is how to deal with the justice of submission.

But we have found—as have many others—that adopting this more complete and balanced view of submission brings a greater unity, love, and fulfillment to marriage.

For me, I found great contentment in Pete's handling of my new understanding of submission. The more I opened up and shared my ideas and plans, the less fear I felt that he would reject them. And he, for his part, sensed a greater responsibility to love and cherish me, listening carefully to what I had to say, since I am a God-given resource for him. His love prevented him from disregarding my feelings and desires. He always took them into consideration, even though his decision sometimes went against my wishes.

Today, Pete encourages me to develop my skills and talents. He does not feel threatened when my gift of teaching takes me away from home, leaving him to take over domestic jobs temporarily. On occasion, he has embarrassed me by being my most enthusiastic "fan." He promotes my ministry as I promote his.

In fact, the best verse to sum up the relationship I believe God wants between a husband and wife is this:

> Submit to one another out of reverence for Christ. (Eph. 5:21)

Some would hold that this verse is referring generally to the whole body of Christ. There is, however, a hierarchy in the church in terms of decision-making and direction. Paul warns leaders not to lord it over those who follow them. And Jesus said that if you want to be the greatest leader, you must be the servant of all. (See Matt. 20:26.)

What the Bible shows us, when we view it as a fabric and not in patches, is a beautiful circle of love. The one in submission, whether in the church or in a marriage, learns to *adapt, be subject to,* and *submit all things* to the leader. The one who is the head learns to listen sensitively to the one in submission, making wise, well-informed, and loving decisions.

Little wonder that Paul likened a marriage to Christ's relationship to His bride, the church. As members of the church, it is not our position to direct our affairs, or to tell Him what is best. We can, through prayer, submit our petitions to Him. And in the end, the authority is His. Though we may not know why He chooses to answer our prayers as He does, we always know that His response is motivated by a holy love.

This is the marvelous picture that Paul intended for us to carry in our hearts as we live and relate as husbands and wives.

After reading these last two chapters, I recommend that you and your spouse sit down and reread them together. Perhaps you'll find that you are right on target in your relationship. More likely, you'll find that there are some areas in which you need to make adjustments. It may require a lot of work.

No matter what it requires, building—or rebuilding—your marriage according to biblical principles is an important goal. Not only is marriage intended to bring incredible joy to us, but it was meant to be an example to the world of Christ's love for the church and our willing servanthood under Him.

And I think both of those goals are worth any price. Don't you?

CHAPTER NINE

THAT THE WORLD MAY KNOW

The principles that God was teaching us in our casual friendships and in our marriages soon began to have a powerful affect on our whole church as a body. And we realized that God was not just blessing us with better, smoother-working relationships just so we could be happy with one another. That was blessing enough—but, as always, God has many purposes weaving together at one time.

Just before His crucifixion, Jesus spoke to His disciples about many things, including the effects their lives could have on the world around them. In John 13:34, 35, He told them:

> A new commandment I give you: Love one another. As I have loved you, so you must love one another. *All men will know that you are my disciples if you love one another* (italics added).

Yes, God wants to take the love we have for

one another and allow it to shine like a beacon in this dark world of confused relationships, anger, bitterness and estrangement. Many of us like the idea of loving one another—so long as we think that love means nice, warm feelings, compliments, and nothing going wrong. God's purpose is that we demonstrate to a world that cannot get along with each other the Holy Spirit's power to bring *unity*. But as we know, it is sometimes hard enough for two individual Christians to live in a right relationship—whether it's friend with friend, or spouse with spouse—much less a church full of people to be rightly related to one another.

How can we become Jesus' disciples—the body of Christ—fulfilling His purpose for us as a community of believers in this world?

As I mentioned, God worked in our church, teaching us lessons about our individual friendships and our marriages—and then began dealing with our inter-relationships as a body of Christians.

The process was something like learning to drive a car with a standard transmission. You start with your left foot pressing on the clutch, while your right foot begins to push the gas pedal. You ease up the clutch and increase pressure on the gas, hoping to strike the right balance so that the engine doesn't shudder and jerk. In the meantime—while your brain is trying to concentrate on your feet—your upper body is trying to do three things at once: keep an eye on the road, steer the car, and coordinate the gearshift. On the first time out, the whole procedure seems impossible.

In a similar way, it may seem impossible to you that a church or a group of believers can coordinate all its various opinions, needs, preferences, and ideas enough to keep relationships rolling smoothly. We had similar misgivings and doubts, especially when a number of people from our church all decided to settle in the same apartment complex in order to live in Christian fellowship throughout the week. They worshiped together on Sunday, and they saw each other all week long. Their kids played together—and sometimes fought; they visited in each others' apartments—and sometimes had disagreements. When they walked out their doors, they bumped into one another. Could they keep up their Christian witness living in such close conditions? Would they wind up even *liking* each other?

What we all learned from this "experiment in agreeable living" has valuable applications for all Christians who want to fulfill Jesus' commandment that we become known to the world by our love for one another. Whether you are involved in a home or "cell" group, or even a regular prayer and Bible study group, the same principles can apply to fit your circumstances.

First, it's important to discuss and verbalize the purpose of a group. This will set the tone and direction. Discuss these questions among yourselves: What is our group's basic purpose? Are we meeting for deep, intimate sharing—or light fellowship? Are we going to minister to one another—or just pray together? Who is in charge of the group for determining the direction of individual meetings or gatherings? How do individuals relate to the leaders if the members have a need or a point of disagreement? Working on answers to these questions can help you avoid misunderstandings.

A couple of points of caution: Don't expect perfect agreement on answers to some of these questions immediately. Be flexible. And above all, learn to disagree agreeably from the very outset. Don't take on a win/lose attitude when making decisions. This mentality will crush the move of the Holy Spirit through individuals in the group. Listen for His voice regarding the purpose of the group, and be willing for His direction to change as time goes on.

Second, it may become necessary to verbalize certain aspects of your commitment to one another. It is *not* necessary to strong-arm people to make a commitment to attend every meeting or risk being considered an outsider. This becomes legalistic and oppressive. Making verbal commitments or agreements with one another is meant to keep channels of communication clear and to avoid misunderstandings and ruptured friendships.

For example, when our friends in the apartment complex decided to live as a community of Christians, they had a number of things to talk out.

One of the women told me, "We made the decision to become a community after hearing teaching on it. We discussed it and literally had brain-storming sessions, looking for ways to develop the groups. We read books like *Living Together in a World Falling Apart*, (Church of the Redeemer, Houston, Tex.)."

One area that needed careful attention was the discipline of their children. This is an area most groups will need to consider. Disagreements arise between couples because each family will naturally have different rules and standards for childrearing. What is considered cause for discipline in a family with stricter standards may not apply in a family that has chosen, for their own private reasons, to be more lenient. Nonetheless, when couples bring their children together in a group setting, some methods of order will make things run more smoothly.

The families in the apartment complex did talk about discipline guidelines when continued problems arose among the children. The general consensus was that an adult in the group had the authority to stop a child caught destroying property or hurting another child. Most parents agreed that an adult could reprimand the child, apart from physical punishment. Then they were to notify the parents. Others felt hesitant about anyone else reprimanding their children; they felt it was a private matter. Knowing these guidelines and preferences helped to greatly minimize friction.

Among our apartment-dwellers, a governing council of three couples was set up for the very reason of settling disputes. In fact, they came to a split-decision on a major issue early on. They decided, however, that they would not move ahead on the issue until they were in complete agreement. Each one on the council agreed to pray and listen for God's voice on the matter.

In the end, they did come to an agreement—and more than that, there was a tremendous sense of love and a witness of God's peace to all the other families. What could have been an ugly disagreement turned into an opportunity to bring glory to God for softening their hearts toward one another.

Another benefit in establishing leadership roles is for group guidance. God often speaks on behalf of others to individuals in the body who are willing to pray and be open to Him. But there is even greater strength and comfort that can come with guidance given by a group of leaders whose calling it is to oversee a group.

Glenn Mattox, who headed the governing council in the apartments, related to me that God sometimes intervened supernaturally, giving special discernment and knowledge.

Once, as Glenn prayed for one of the couples, he began to feel uneasy. He had the clear impression that their marriage was in trouble. He continued to pray and seek God until he knew he must confront the husband.

Looking the man straight in the eye, Glenn said, "I believe God has shown me that there is difficulty in your marriage because of a certain decision you have made. You've decided that you no longer love your wife!"

Astonished, the man could not hide the truth. As he and Glenn talked, they were able to deal with some roots of the marital problem. And healing began to come into the relationship.

Yet another reason for developing leadership in a group is to see to the discipling of new Christians, and to improve practical care for one another.

Living in an apartment next to one of the church families was a young, unmarried couple. Some of the Christian men led this young man to Christ, and through him the young woman also gave her heart to Jesus. Immediately, they were married—and the task of guiding and instructing them in how to live the Christian life began.

In this case, the Christian couple who lived next door to them suggested that the two families share the evening meal together, alternating between apartments. During these meals, conversations centered on the Bible and the Christian life. This arrangement went on for several months, until the young couple was firmly established in the Christian faith.

The situations in your group will likely be different, but the same principles apply. Jesus told us to "make disciples of all men . . . teaching them to observe whatever I have commanded you" (Matt. 28:19, 20). Too often, we let new Christians "fall between the cracks" when they need strong guidance and help in their spiritual life. Group leaders can and should pick up the challenge to be sure the needs of these new babes in Christ are met.

Earlier, in looking at the biblical principle from Gal. 6:2, where the Apostle Paul says that we are to "carry one another's burdens, and in this way . . . fulfill the law of Christ," which is His commandment to love one another, we applied it to emotional needs. The same principle applies in the context of Christian groups, with regard to bearing one another's practical/physical needs.

Having leadership that is sensitive to the needs of individuals is a true blessing to any group or church. We sometimes lose new Christians because we fail to see that they are discipled, and older Christians often get discouraged when they encounter difficulties, and find no brother or sister there to lend a hand. This is where the ministry of service to others is needed. (See Romans 12 and 1 Corinthians 12.) That is, people who have a genuine heart for the needs of others.

How do you identify someone who has a true servant's heart, who can be relied on to help meet the practical needs of others? This type of person will pick up on casual comments, such as, "We'd really like to go out for ice cream with the group—but money's a little tight for us right now," or "My wife's having a tough time emotionally after this new baby," or "Bill needs a job," or "My mother is dying of cancer, and she's come to live with us. She sure is lonely for visitors." The servants among us are the ones who tune into these comments because they hear with their hearts. Immediately, they think of ways these practical needs can be met. Whether or not they can meet a need themselves or know the right people to call to get things done, they are motivated by a strong desire to see that practical needs are met in the body of Christ.

Among our church families, love in the body was tested when a young mother, Phyllis Sanchez, was confined to bed for the last two months of her pregnancy. It was amazing to see the servants who got to work immediately, organizing a plan to help the Sanchezes. Late each morning, one woman would arrive with lunch for two. She would visit with Phyllis briefly, then do light housework. To cover supper, we arranged a schedule among the other women in the church. In the late afternoon, one of us would carry in a hot meal for the family. There was also laundry and other housework, which was attended to regularly. Even after little Amber was born, the family's needs were cared for during Phyllis's recovery.

In an even more unusual experience Pete and I wondered if the concern of the Body would stretch far enough to meet the needs. Frank and Gloria Wilson, a few years older than most in the church, were looked upon by many as Mom and Dad figures. Frank had worked many years at Uniroyal, but now his union was on strike. During the Sunday morning service the Wilsons' need was mentioned only casually to the congregation: "Frank's on strike, folks; I don't think I have to say any more."

I wondered if enough had been said. Shouldn't we have been reminded of our responsibility to one another? Surely that was not enough to bring the response needed. Or had the Lord prompted Pete to say no more to the congregation?

During our prayer time together the next morning, Pete and I discussed the Wilsons' situation. They had told us they had a small savings that could carry them for a few weeks, but they had no resources beyond that. We wondered what we should do to prompt the congregation to assist them, yet we had a strong sense that we should do nothing.

Frank took whatever work he could find in the coming weeks, but it was not enough. The Wilsons were wondering if they should put their home up for sale rather than fall behind in payments.

Six weeks into the strike, when their savings were depleted and there was no prospect of income, God tested their obedience and they saw His faithfulness. Gloria felt God wanted her to give then dollars to a radio ministry as an expression of faith that God would provide their needs. After making the pledge, she wondered if she had done the right thing.

The next day Gloria's neighbor asked if she would be interested in a part-time job. And the following day a check for $100 arrived in the mail from a young Christian couple.

The Wilsons arrived at church the next Sunday to find sacks of groceries had been set to one side with their name on them. No one saw them placed there, and no one admitted to it.

The strike went on for weeks and we wondered how the Wilsons' needs would be met. I began to look forward to Gloria's phone calls giving an update on their adventure. One morning they answered the doorbell of their mobile home to find no one there, but at their feet was a supply of meat, fresh from someone's freezer, cheering them on.

Occasionally the union strike was mentioned in prayer from the pulpit, but as far as we know, there was no organized effort to minister to Frank and Gloria's needs. Sometimes their house fellowship leader delivered boxes of food and supplies that had been brought to him so that the givers could remain anonymous. The sharing of food and money was coming from brothers and sisters in the Lord who saw a need and responded to the biblical instruction to meet that need according to their abilities.

As the strike stretched on into its third and fourth months, Pete and I watched with growing wonder. Would the people reach a saturation point and stop extending help to the Wilsons? Again and again the church treasurer found offerings designated for them, or they would find money in their mailbox.

One Sunday rejoicing erupted after Gloria stood at her place in the third pew to report that the strike had finally ended after four and a half months. She tearfully and joyfully expressed their thanks to God for His faithfulness, and thanks to their church family who had shared their love and sustenance. We later learned that

Gloria had recorded in a notebook over $1800 in cash, plus the many gifts of food and other help given by the church family. We were amazed. All of that had followed only one brief mention from the pulpit. No organized effort had been made to meet these needs, yet the Wilsons had not missed a house payment nor been threatened with loss of utilities or phone service.

It is this kind of care and attention given to the Wilson and Sanchez families that will help the body of Christ to grow strong and loving. Observing, non-believers will say, "These people are true disciples of Jesus Christ. Look at the tremendous love they have for each other."

Jesus gave another admonition that applies to the growth in numbers among our Christian groups. In Jesus' great priestly prayer for all believers throughout time, He prayed that the love of His followers would be so tremendous "that the world may believe that [God the Father] has sent me."

In other words, Jesus prayed that our unified love would be so great that it would splash over the boundaries of our own groups, soaking the world with care and kindness. God's love was never meant to be hoarded among God's children. He wants us to pour it out on the needy who do not yet know Him.

We've been focusing on a group of believers from our church who chose to live in close proximity in order to illustrate biblical principles in small-group dynamics. Now we turn our attention to the impact in our community when our church decided to act on the principle of John 17. As with commitments made *within* the body, we learned that it is important to evaluate commitments made to people *outside* the church or group. It is easy to look at the needs all around us, be overwhelmed by the vast numbers of people who need our help, and therefore do nothing. It is also easy, on the other hand, to be carried away with exuberance and make commitments beyond what we can fulfill.

In determining what your commitment will be, consider Jesus' directive to His disciples when He told them that the wise disciple—and one who sticks with his commitments—is the one who counts the cost first. (See Luke 14:25–35.) But once you've counted the cost—*step out and be the servant of Jesus Christ!*

For us, it took a series of events, in the mid-seventies, to teach us the concept of the Christian community as a servant-witness to the world.

Shortly after the fall of Saigon, we learned that thousands of Vietnamese were waiting at nearby Camp Pendleton for relocation. Only those who had sponsors would be released to find homes and seek employment. Pete and I made a preliminary visit to the camp, where we were met by a sea of eager Asian faces. Their pleading looks betrayed what they could not say in English: "Please help me to leave here."

Then we seemed to be led to one family, the Phans. Their extended "family" included the wife's sister and brother, plus another girl whom they considered a family member. Seven people in all. Only the father, Phan Tan Hung, spoke any English, which he spoke fairly well. What kind of commitment would it take to help these people? Would our congregation be willing to make such a commitment? We knew too much about body relationships to take a decision like this for granted, or to move ahead without counting the cost.

We needn't have worried about enthusiasm—there was no lack of it. By the next Sunday, word had spread that Pete and I had a family in mind. We did not take this enthusiasm as a green light, however.

At the end of the service, Pete led in a prayer asking the Lord to give us wisdom in making the right decision. We wanted to be God's servants to work out whatever plan He had in mind for the lives of these refugees. We also had a meeting following the service, during which anyone could voice objections, questions, or make comments about the venture. After all, we were talking about the lives of people. And the conclusion we came to was this: If Pete and I were willing to house the family for the immediate future, the congregation would commit themselves to finding clothes, household items, and six months' rent to cover an apartment for the Phan family when housing was located. In the meantime, the men would also be searching for the right job for the father.

So our church did choose to sponsor the Phan family, and we brought them home to live with us. The unified outpouring of care and provision was truly a witness to the love of Christ for these homeless people. We learned to pronounce strange-sounding words and names so we could communicate, and soon were transporting the adults and teenagers to English language classes. We taught them how to shop in American stores. The congregation brought gifts of food and meals, clothes and genuine friendship. Eventually, the Phans were able to find employment and housing, and we continued to help them adjust to life in our American culture.

Most importantly, we witnessed signs that lasting relationships with the Phan family were being built. During a short period of time, two women in our congregation, Nyla and Denise, both delivered still-born babies. The next time Fung, the mother of our Vietnamese family, saw Denise, she pointed at Denise's stomach and began to weep. Though these two women were separated by language and cultural barriers, their heartbreak was a common bond at the death of a child. Even through tragedy, God was forging bonds of love.

What we learned from these experiences was vast. I want to share a few significant and practical principles that will help your groups as you commit to becoming a witness to the world by a practical show of love.

I have already talked about verbalizing your commitment. And I want to reemphasize: *Think thoroughly through the commitment you have made to help others.* Or, as Jesus put it, count the cost. Know that there may come a time, after you've made the commitment in a moment of excitement and inspiration, when the feelings are gone and the commitment is still staring you in the face. Literally! Then you will need to rely on the patience and perseverance of the Holy Spirit in you to fulfill your work in Christ to the end of the task.

There is one most important area, when it comes to this business of our love-witness as a group, that is often overlooked. Pete and I learned about this special principle in a way that imprinted it indelibly on our hearts.

When we began to draw closer together as a body of Christians, there were a few who felt somewhat uncomfortable at first. Everyone understood that we were not attempting to have control over individuals or families, which is a cultic practice, and soon all became involved to greater or lesser degrees in the effort to live by biblical principles. All, it seemed, except one family.

This family had moved to our area about a year before our emphasis on relationships began, and they attended Sunday services regularly. But we never saw them between Sundays unless someone made a special visit. They seemed to be holding back. Pete decided a pastoral call was in order, to find out if there was some problem preventing them from entering into the life of the church.

Pete spoke frankly about the desire God had given him to see all the members living by these principles. After hearing Pete out, the man responded.

"I've been a part of this body since the first

week we came," he said. "Every morning at 2:30, the Lord wakens me to pray for every family in the church by name. God frequently shares with me specific needs—which I hear about only later from others.

"The Lord has also shared with me trials that you and Bev are going through sometimes," he went on. "I intercede for you, and later I hear you talk about the very things I've been praying for."

By now, the man was weeping. "I'm sorry that we've not been as openly active in this body as you've wanted. Will you forgive me?"

Pete, feeling about two inches tall and close to tears himself, replied, "There's nothing to forgive, brother. I'm the one who's been wrong. I've judged you as not having a commitment to this church family, when you're as much a part of us as anyone else. Will you forgive me?"

Restoration of the relationship came.

I tell this story in closing this chapter to make a final point: Participation in God's family can take many forms. Often, the unseen member is making just as tremendous a contribution as the one who is highly visible and involved all the time.

Let us remember, in our activity for God, that every one of our actions in His name must be rooted and grounded in the activity of prayer. For it's not our kingdom we are building. And only as the mind of Christ directs our actions can we truly make the faith declaration: "May your kingdom come and your will be done, on earth as it is in heaven."

CHAPTER TEN

ACCOUNTABILITY, EQUALITY, AND AUTHORITY

There are few things more needed today among Christians than a clear understanding of the biblical principles of accountability, equality, and authority.

We've begun to grasp the principles that will give us strong, true relationships with fellow Christians and with our spouses. And yet, when it comes to understanding our proper relationship *within* a body, we hit snags. Many Christians bristle when their pastors suggest that they need to take better control of their children, or their finances, or their moral standards. Christian groups often wind up in a tussle between two or more strong personalities because each feels he has gifts and callings that qualify him for leadership.

Most of us are influenced by a worldly and humanistic society. Few men and women today recognize a higher authority than themselves. We demand our rights and refuse to have anyone rule over us. This attitude is partly incited by the failure of government, civic, and even Christian leaders. It's true that there is a crisis in leadership today.

Individuals generally fear making themselves accountable to leaders (which is a form of submission) because they don't want to be duped or taken advantage of. Beyond that, an independent spirit results in numerous splits and fractures in the body of Christ. Even the choice of leaders is often based on the desire to hear what is comfortable to hear.

These are strong words, I know, and they are not spoken in a judgmental spirit. But I want to arrest your attention, and get you to think about a warning that came from one of the greatest church leaders in history.

The Apostle Paul, dismayed by the factions and striving for power in the Corinthian church, wrote these sobering words:

> Brothers, I could not address you as spiritual but as *worldly*—mere infants in Christ. . . . For since there is jealousy and quarreling among you, are you not worldly? . . . For when one of you says, "I follow Paul," and another says, "I follow Apollos," are you not mere men? (1 Cor. 3:1, 3–4, emphasis added)

Paul went on in that chapter and the next (1 Cor. 4) to talk quite bluntly about the kind of Christian leaders that Christians *should* follow.

Guided by the Holy Spirit in writing this and other Scripture passages, Paul—who was commissioned by God to establish His church—had a lot to say about the balance of accountability, equality, and authority. If we want to live in a body of Christians that demonstrates biblical balance, we need to understand these three principles.

Perhaps the most basic need in this regard is the need to understand *accountability*.

Some time after Pete had begun to teach on this subject, a man named Charles approached him nervously one day. He talked about many subjects, while Pete, sensing that something was "up," waited for Charles to zero-in. Finally, he got to the point.

"I've never expressed this before, Pete, but I want to be accountable to you as my pastor. Though in my heart I knew it was the scriptural thing to do, I never got around to it. I guess I was afraid."

"What were you afraid of?" Pete asked.

"Well," Charles replied thoughtfully, "I know you would never force your will on me and that you have my best interests at heart. I guess it's just the idea of giving up my independence."

Later, Pete had a good chuckle as he related the conversation. Charles is one of the most self-controlled individuals we know, not a self-willed person who's always doing something foolish or daring from which he needs to be held back. Of all people to be concerned about accountability!

Yet the fear persists—and not without cause.

Two extremes exist in the church when it comes to the area of being accountable (or subject) to authority. One stream, as we've said, takes the attitude, "Pastor, my Christian life is a private matter between me and God, and you have no business nosing into my personal life; stick to teaching about 'spiritual' things." The other stream takes the position that group or church members must give control of their lives to a leader-governor whose "authority" verges on dictatorship. This dictator dispenses direction for every area of individual life.

With these two misconceptions so prevalent, it's no wonder that Christians are usually accountable to no one, or turned-off altogether by the concept.

Obviously, each individual is responsible for seeking God's direction for himself. Nonetheless, accountability is a scriptural principle. Paul and Jesus both taught that there were to be overseers, or "shepherds," over the "flock." These leaders are to be regarded with respect "as those entrusted with the secret things of God" (1 Cor. 4:1). It is to these men, whom God entrusts with His secrets, that we are to entrust ourselves. This is God's ordained system of order for His people.

By why is this system even necessary?

Prov. 11:14 gives us the first reason: *"Advisers make victory sure."*

One of God's good gifts to us is the care and concern of godly leaders who will commit themselves to prayer on our behalf. When we are emotionally or spiritually confused, when we are wrapped up in circumstances that are sinking us, it is truly a blessing to have someone to whom we can turn.

Counselors, pastors, and group leaders will know what I mean by "spiritual butterflies"—people who flit from one adviser to another, searching for a "right" answer to their particular problem. Unfortunately, these people usually accept no answer. This is often because they do not want to be accountable for the advice given and the personal changes that are subsequently required. If you know people like this, pray that their eyes will be opened to their own behavior.

A second reason for accountability is that God intends that we have transparent relationships (which we discussed at length earlier) leading to healthy intimacy built on trust.

In 1 Pet. 5:5 we are told that we should be submitted to those in authority over us. We have found it best if you *verbalize* this commitment to your pastor or elder. Let me explain why this is so necessary:

When you go to a doctor, for instance, you tell him your symptoms, and there is an implied commitment of trust: "I'm entrusting my health to you, believing that you will advise me correctly, and administer the right treatment for my ailment, helping me to recover, no matter what it takes."

Why do we see the care and well-being of our souls as any less important than the care of our bodies? It is every bit as important, and the leader you are seeking out for advice and prayer ought to know whether you are serious about finding God's solution to your question, no matter what it takes. Few things are more discouraging to a pastor than to pour his heart and his time into a hurting member of the congregation, only to have that person walk away without trusting his counsel.

You can, and *should*, tell your spiritual leader the areas of your life with which you trust him. Tell him you will also pray for him and his family and their needs. And along with that, especially concerning your pastor, see that his material needs are being met adequately. Be a giver of blessings as well as a receiver.

Along with being accountable to leaders, God intends us to accept wisdom from other members of the body. God has made each of us priests (see Heb. 4:16), with access to God's throne room through prayer. We should never take the prayerful counsel of another lightly. Our Christian brothers and sisters, like our leaders, are able to confirm insights and directions God is trying to show us. Those who are not open to any guidance or correction from others are in danger of turning inward and becoming unteachable.

But are we to submit to Christian authority or the counsel of a Christian brother even if we sense there is something "off" about their advice?

No. Even spiritual leaders can, as the Apostle Peter, speak revelatory words from God one moment and words from Satan the next. Words of guidance spoken to us by others are always to be weighed in light of God's Word and our own relationship with the Father. Authority can and should be tested. It must not be domineering, leading to bondage or dependence, but should be freeing, fulfilling, and life-giving. God holds each of us accountable for his own actions. If a leader tells you it is okay to lie or cheat and you do so, both come under God's judgment (Eccles. 12:14).

One of the factors that confuses the issue of relationships in the body of Christ is the question of *equality*. Doesn't the Bible say that we are all equal? The answer is yes!

The Bible clearly teaches that we are all equal. Equality, in fact, is a part of the very nature of God, who, being three distinct persons—Father, Son and Holy Spirit—is nevertheless one. Because there is a God, we can say each human being has inherent value before Him. And regarding the body of Christ, Paul tells us, "There is neither Jew nor Greek . . . bond nor free . . . male nor female; for you are all one in Christ Jesus" (Gal. 3:28).

In one sense, there is total equality before God in the body of Christ:

> The body is a unit, though it is made up of many parts; and though all its parts are many, they form one body. So it is with Christ. (1 Cor. 12:12).

Paul then goes on at some length to paint a word picture of a physical body in which eyes and hands are arguing over which of them is more important—providing a bit of humor for his readers along with the spiritual insight.

Frequently, an attitude of superiority arises in a Christian who believes his office or gift makes him a more important part of the body. These unfortunate people are easily wounded when others don't accept their "authority." They cannot understand why Christian brothers and sisters, and even their own pastor, don't turn the whole church around in the direction they believe it should go. But the fact is they are part of a body— an equal member, to be sure, but still needing to have an attitude of accountability and submission to the wisdom of all the other members.

Only when our insistence on equality makes us humble and not demanding will we properly view our relationships to one another. I believe that God will not release spiritual authority to an individual until he understands equality and the proper functioning of the body. You are spiritually ready for Him to elevate you to a position of leadership when you can say, "My job in the body is equally important in God's eyes to any other job. Different maybe, but equal." If someone insists on having authority without recognizing and practicing true humility, his motives for wanting to be in leadership are coming from a source other than God.

Spiritual authority comes in the same way the Father released authority to His own Son. Jesus said, "I can do nothing on my own initiative, because I do not seek my will" (John 5:30; see also 6:38; 7:16–17). Authority is available to us only under the same conditions: *submission and obedience to the will of God.*

What are the attributes of the person who is called to have spiritual authority over others? And what are his responsibilities?

The first attribute that is imperative for a Christian leader in his relationships with others is to recognize the principle in Heb. 13:17. A leader who understands authority is one who knows he is called to watch over the souls of others because he will one day have to stand before God and give an account for those who were under his care (Heb. 13:17).

One who holds spiritual authority must recognize that he, too, is accountable. First, as Hebrews says, he is accountable to God. It is from God's Word, then, that a leader draws His authority. First Peter reveals several of the principles that should guide a leader:

> Be shepherds of God's flock that is under your care, serving as overseers—not because you must, but because you are willing, as God wants you to be. (1 Pet. 5:2)

The leader who is leading God's way not only knows that others are given into his care, but he sees himself as their *chief servant*. In his heart is the desire to be able to empower his flock to be what God intends them to be, not that they should make him great, or wealthy, or powerful. He willingly does this, because he know this is his job in the body—helping to release others into their gifts and callings. Seeing someone come to freedom, or seeing him fulfilled in Christ is one of the true leader's greatest joys.

Further in the same passage in Peter, we read about two other principles that are to govern the spirit of one in authority:

> . . . not lording it over those entrusted to you
> but being examples to the flock. (1 Pet. 5:3)

The one in authority is not a lord, one who must be obeyed without question. Those leaders who insist on this brand of submission come dangerously close to a cultic mind-set, or at the least they are very immature.

One in authority is also put there as an example of godliness, correctly representing Christ to His bride, the church. A leader is one whose life, love, words, and actions all say, "This is what Christ is like." A very high calling, indeed.

A leader is to be in relationship with other spiritual leaders (Eph. 5:21; Acts 20:28). In this way, he keeps himself spiritually in-tune with what God is doing in the church at large; he listens to what the Spirit is saying to the churches (Revelation 1—3), and he keeps himself in balance by checking his personal life, his ideas and directions against the experience and counsel of other leaders. Just as God did not intend there to be "Lone Ranger" Christians, He also did not intend there to be "Lone Ranger" leaders.

Finally, a spiritual leader is to give correction where needed, but it is to be loving correction. Paul put it best when he wrote:

> Brothers, if someone is caught in a sin, you
> who are spiritual should restore him gently.

But watch yourself, or you also may be tempted. (Gal. 6:1)

At first glance, it may seem as though Paul is only telling leaders to be gentle in restoring the person who has been overtaken by sin. Certainly the good shepherd—emulating *the* Good Shepherd—will leave the ninety-nine sheep in order to rescue the lost one and bind up his wounds. But the second part of the verse may also be taken as a warning, and one to which leaders today should pay careful attention.

I believe Paul is warning leaders to guard themselves in their relationships, even those pertaining to ministry. Many times we hear about the desperate young woman who seeks her pastor's comfort during a time of marital trouble—only to be seduced. But what about the Christian leaders—men and women alike—who fall prey to those seeking "counsel." Too many Christian leaders, at conferences, retreats and even in church offices, have found themselves pushed into compromising positions, or have yielded to offers that appealed to some area of weakness. Yes, there are casualties on both sides.

A leader must keep in mind that he is there to represent the truth—which is Jesus Christ. He is not to try to *be* truth, the eternal answer-man to all needs, the healer of all hurts. Like other human beings, he has needs. And that is why God has placed him, just like every other believer, in a body.

We have had a rounded-out picture of body

relationships. Making yourself accountable does not mean you become a slave. It means protection, guidance, and recognizing responsibilities. Holding authority does not make you a lord; it makes you chief servant, one who is called to lift others up, not keep them down.

Yes, we are equal before God. But He has also asked that we live by the principles of accountability and authority. These two are opposite sides of the same coin. And the coin has value only when its worth means this to all involved: *A loving commitment to one another.*

CHAPTER ELEVEN

THE HIGHEST AIM

Perhaps you've been challenged by the principles for biblical relationships that we've looked at in this book, or by the experiences we went through as a church. My hope, of course, is that you'll want to begin applying these principles in your life and in the groups with which you're involved.

You may also be asking, "Where do I begin?"

Let me give you some thoughts, as we close, on how to start the process of change.

First, do not sit back and wait for someone else to start living according to biblical relationship principles. You must choose to be that one person who willingly serves God, no strings attached. Make your commitment the same as that of the unknown hymn writer who penned these inspiring words: "I have decided to follow Jesus. . . . No turning back, no turning back!"

Remember that your first and most important relationship is with Jesus Christ, our Lord. And as He told His first-century followers:

You are the salt of the earth. . . . You are the
light of the world. A city on a hill cannot be
hidden. Neither do people light a lamp and
put it under a bowl. Instead they put it on its
stand, and it gives light to everyone in the
house. In the same way, let your light shine
before men that they may see your good
deeds and praise your Father in heaven.
(Matt. 5:13–16)

Your decision to put these truths into practice should not be hindered by a fear that others
may think you've got a "holier-than-thou" attitude. When you make the commitment to let
God's Word shine through in all your relationships, with His help, then you will become salt and
light, flavoring and enlightening all those with
whom you come in contact.

Secondly, don't try to apply all the principles
in this book at once. We did not learn these lessons
all at once, nor can you.

Start right where you are, with the friends
and family God has given you and in whatever
church you attend. You may first want to make a
commitment to become "principle-conscious."
Ask God to help you to see other principles in His
Word that may apply more specifically in your
life. Bible reading becomes more exciting when
you begin to look for principles taught or lived
by the men and women in the Scriptures. Ask
God, too, to open your eyes for opportunities to
apply what you are learning.

You may also wish to ask a brother or sister
in Christ, or your spouse, to enter into a covenant-

agreement with you. You can begin with two principles: "Go to your brother if you have ought . . ." and "speaking the truth in love."

Do not *push* these principles on anyone. You cannot force intimacy. Learn to discover God's timing as well as His method. Keep in mind that "the letter kills, but the Spirit gives life" (2 Cor. 2:6). If we try to operate in these principles without the Spirit of God showing us how, we will lack the breath of God that must infill all of our efforts to give them life.

Don't neglect the Old Testament in your search for biblical relationship principles. We must never negate the importance of this major portion of Scripture by using the line, "I'm a New Testament Christian, under grace, not the law."

The concept of living by principles originated in the Old Testament. The New Testament tells us that God has written the Ten Commandments on our hearts (Rom. 2:15). When we know the Old Testament, we can carry out God's absolutes. Then we are free; we have the law of liberty (James 1:25).

Most important, memorize 1 Corinthians 13—the "Love Chapter." Love is to be our highest aim.

Love underlies the best in every relationship. The community God built in His church is knit together with the yarn of love, a love that Christ put in our hearts for one another. Ask God to fill your heart with love. For the love of Christ is the only motivation that can empower one to live the true Christ-life.

If, for instance, we go to a brother who has offended us, confronting him with a self-righteous attitude, we are only using a biblical principle for hurtful purposes. Hearing someone tell you the truth about yourself, without the soothing balm of love added, is not only hurtful but may be destructive to the soul. Acceptance without love is just tolerance. Our motive should be to build up a brother or sister in their faith toward God—never to mold them in our image.

The Apostle Paul wrote, "My prayer for you is that you will overflow more and more with love for others" (Phil. 1:9a, TLB). Our love is not to be stagnant, or confined to just a few. And what kind of love was Paul referring to? The same kind that he instructed the Corinthians to have: a love that is patient, humble, believing in others and enduring hard times.

At the same time, our love is not to be like cotton candy—sweet fluff, without substance. Paul also says we are to "keep on growing in spiritual knowledge and insight, for I want you always to see clearly the difference between right and wrong, and to be inwardly clean" (Phil. 1:9b, 10, TLB). Here, Paul links spiritual knowledge and insight to right living and purity. Likewise, in Titus 2:1, he refers to the person who has "sound doctrine" as the one whose character reflects temperance, patience and, yes, love for others.

I close with this prayer, offered by the Apostle Paul in Phil. 1:11:

May you always be doing those good, kind

things which show that you are a child of God, for this will bring much praise and glory to the Lord. (TLB)

That is my prayer for you, too!